I0480301

# The Olympus E-M10 MkIIl Menu System Simplified

**by David Thorpe**

**Published in the United Kingdom**

**First Publishing Date March 2019**

# Introduction

Perhaps the Olympus E-M10 MkIII is your first digital camera or just upgraded from a point and shoot or phone camera? Or maybe you've just been idly scanning through the menu options on your E-M10 MkIII and thought "I wonder what that does"? The menu system and controls of the E-M10 MkIII are well presented and thoughtfully implemented but necessarily complex. With six sections containing multitude of menu items, even the experienced user will sometimes find themselves scratching their head and wondering what an entry means. This small book goes through every menu choice and control and explains (a) what it does and (b) why you might want to do it. It may not inspire you in a literary sense but with its help you may find a E-M10 MkIII tailored to your personal taste inspiring to use. I sometimes give my opinion on the best setting. It is only my opinion from my personal experience. It is best treated it as merely a starting point for building your own experience. At the end of the book I go though the menu items as I set them. The aim of this is to give you a working setup without having to learn what each item does straight away. As you use the camera with my settings you will find yourself thinking, "that's really annoying. If only I could change that." You most likely can. Find the item in question and change it. You now have a E-M10 MkIII a little more tailored to you than before. The aim, eventually, is to have a photographic tool that is personal to your needs. The Olympus E-M10 MkIII is a versatile and effective photographic tool. Time spent learning what the Olympus E-M10 MkIII can do and how to do it will be rewarded by better pictures. And that, after all, is why you bought it!

*(Errors or comments contact me at books@dthorpe.net)*

# Starter Notes

Even though the operation of the Olympus E-M10 MkIII has been designed to be as easy as possible, the complexity of such a sophisticated digital camera means it cannot be used to its full potential without some understanding of the underlying technology. Here, for those who don't have a background in the art (yet!) is a brief rundown of the main terms and principles it is necessary to know. I have based this

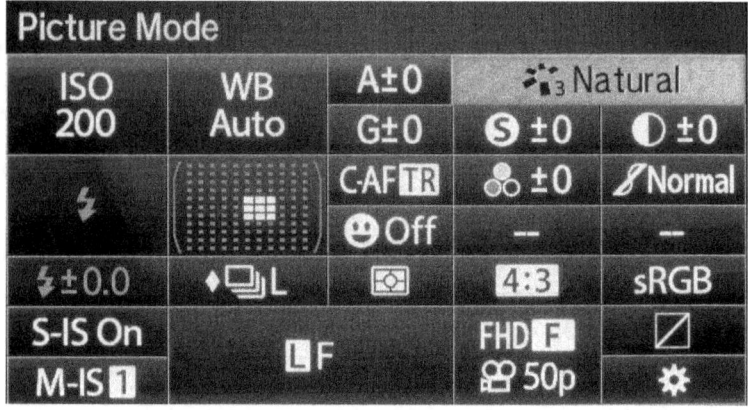

page on the settings available in the **Super Control Panel** The taking of a technically acceptable photograph needs two main functions to be mastered, exposure and focus. The wonder of the digital camera is the multitude of tools at your disposal to control these functions.**Note:** exposure changes are often spoken about in **stops**. A **stop** is a represents a doubling or halving of exposure, so if you were shooting at 1/500th at f/8 and wanted to give an extra stop of exposure, you could shoot at 1/250th at f/8 or 1/500th at f/5.6. Both would let twice the amount of light onto the sensor. **Note:** Historically, a stop represents the click stops on the lens aperture ring at, say f/1.4, f/2, f/2.8 and so on, each of which represents a doubling or halving of the exposure depending on which direction you move the ring. Nowadays it is used generically as a term for describing the amount by which you are changing exposure even if you do it by changing the shutter speed. Many (most) modern lenses don't have a physical aperture ring but use one of the camera's controls, usually a front or rear dial, to take over the task.

## **Exposure**

The image sensor of a digital camera requires a certain amount of light for a correct exposure. Not enough and the picture is too dark, too much and it is too light. The amount of light hitting the sensor can be controlled in two ways, by varying the shutter speed or by varying the lens aperture.**Note:** if at any time the exposure required is beyond the range of the current camera settings, the shutter speed or aperture display will flash. If the light is too bright for the settings available (unlikely), you will need what are know as ND filters (neutral density). These are filters that do much the same as good sunglasses, they absorb excess light while not affecting the colour. If the light is too dim, then bring the flash into action.

## **Shutter Speed**

is straightforward enough in that if the shutter says open for 1/250th of a second it will let through half as much light as a speed of 1/125th and twice as much as a shutter speed of 1/500th. The E-M10 MkIII offers a range of shutter speeds from 60 seconds to 1/4000th which would cover the vast majority of subjects from the darkest night scene to the brightest sunlight. For sports you need a shutter speed of 1/500th or faster to stop the action while for someone walking at a normal pace a 1/125th or 1/250th will suffice. Movement is less noticeable for subjects moving towards or away from the camera, much more so for subjects moving across the field of view. A show jumping pic where the photographer is placed head on to the jump might show adequate sharpness even at 1/125th whereas with the horse moving across the file of view you'd need an absolute minimum of 1/500th. For slower shutter speeds that you might use in dim light or with immobile subjects there is a rule of thumb that the lowest speed hand-holdable to obtain decent sharpness is twice the focal length of the lens. Thus, a 200mm lens requires a minimum shutter speed of 1/400th. When stabilization comes into the equation, you can safely lower that by at least 3 stops, so a hand held 200mm lens can be used at 1/50th with sharp results. Obviously these recommendations are subject to how steady the photographer's hands are.

## **Aperture**

This is simply the hole in the lens through which light reaches the sensor. Its size governs how much light reaches the sensor. In principle, the aperture is the focal length of the lens divided by the width of the front element of them lens. So, a 25mm standard lens for Micro Four Thirds which had a front element 12.5mm across would be a 25/12.5 = 2, (written f/2) lens and f/2 would be the maximum aperture. Maximum aperture is colloquially referred to as 'wide open' or 'open aperture'. Lenses are fitted internally with an iris diaphragm, a method of narrowing the aperture in effect analogous to the human eye's iris. By making the iris diaphragm narrower, you let a smaller amount of light through and so help control the quantity of light reaching the sensor. The sequence of whole stops for an f/1.4 lens goes f/1.4 f/2 f/2.8 f/4 f/5.6 f/8 f/11 f/16 and occasionally f/22. Each step represents a doubling or halving of the light transmitted, with the smallest number representing the maximum and the bigger the minimum amount. If the latter seems unintuitive, recall how it is calculated. The fewer times the diameter of the lens front glass will divide into its focal length, the bigger it must be - f/1 being a lens where the front element is so wide it will only divide into the focal length once. The fastest lenses available are f/0.95 maximum aperture. A secondary effect of aperture is that the smaller it is, ie the bigger the number, the greater the **Depth of Field**. This is the amount of the subject that is in focus. For a portrait, to draw attention to the subject, it is good to have shallow depth of field, the person in sharp focus, the background out of focus - so use a lens's wide aperture, f/2, say. For a landscape with flowers in the foreground use a smaller aperture, maybe f/8. You could go past f/8 to f/11 or even f/16 for maximum depth of field but it is best not to since an effect known as **diffraction** comes into play. This is a softening of the image overall, taking away the crispness, the critical sharpness. It happens because as the aperture gets smaller and smaller in diameter, it starts to act like a pinhole, making its own very fuzzy image which interferes with the image the glass is making.

## <u>ISO</u>

This stands for International Standards Organisation but in photography has come to mean the measure of the sensitivity to light of a sensor. While the **shutter speed** and **aperture** control the quantity of light hitting the sensor, on their own they are sometimes not enough. What if you have your lens at its maximum aperture and the shutter speed at the lowest you can hand hold but the image will still be under-exposed, too dark? You can increase the **ISO** of the sensor, that is to say its sensitivity to light. So you have an exposure of 1/10th at f/2, your lens's maximum aperture and the **ISO** is at 200. You are worried your hand isn't steady enough to hold the camera still at 1/10th so increase the **ISO** to 400. Now you can shoot at 1/20th @ f/2 and get a well exposed result. It's not all good news, though because while you have a better exposure, the process of increasing the **ISO** introduces noise, a coloured, gritty effect on your image. All increasing **ISO** does is amplify the light on the sensor. In doing so, it amplifies any noise present too, much like turning up the volume on a weak radio transmission.

## Shutter Speed/Aperture/ISO

All three of these things interact with one another and that interaction must be taken into account when choosing them. Lets say you are photographing a parked car on a dullish day. You are using **Aperture Priority** mode and the **ISO** is set to 200. If you set the aperture to f/5.6 the E-M10 MkIII might set a shutter speed of f/125th. That's fine, the car is stationary. The car starts to move off. You don't want a blurred picture so you need to increase the shutter speed. So, open the lens up from f/5.6 to f/4. That doubles the amount of light on the sensor but your picture won't be over-exposed because your camera has registered the one stop aperture change and doubling of the light intensity and immediately speeds up the shutter to 1/250th, halving the light as compared to 1/125th. Thus, the amount of light falling on the sensor remains the same.

If you now up the **ISO** to 400, doubling the sensitivity, the sensor only requires half as much light for a correct exposure. If you leave your aperture at f/4, the sensor will have twice the light it requires and the E-M10 MkIII will compensate by upping the shutter speed to 1/500th. In the end, the exposure setting you need has to be one that gives adequate depth if field, a shutter speed fast enough to stop a moving subject or prevent camera shake and an ISO setting that allows a suitable exposure while not adding too much noise and spoiling the picture. It sounds like a mine field but learning to manipulate these basic controls to most pictorial effect is the basis of photographic technique and a big part of the pleasure of it.

## The AF (AutoFocusing) Area

the E-M10 MkIII has an effective **AF** system with some choice within it. The full grid **All Targets** area lets you leave it to the camera to choose where to focus. This is quite effective for casual use but the camera cannot read your mind so while it mostly finds the best place to focus, it cannot be 100%. You can touch the monitor to give it a bit of guidance, if you wish. There is also a smaller **9-Target Group** array. By reducing the area the camera must scan for likely focusing points, accuracy is greatly improved. This especially applies for sports pictures where a fast changing scene makes focusing complex. Restricting the area the camera must survey greatly increases the efficacy of its decision making. The most accurate focusing comes from using the **Single Target** point. It would be nice to use this all the time but in practice keeping the small focus area box accurately on a fast moving bird or footballer can be next to impossible and the 9-Target grid is a good compromise. There are two ways of using the **Single Target**. Firstly, You can compose your picture and then move the target point to the position where you want to place focus by touching the screen or using the **Arrow** keys. Secondly, leave the target area in the centre, move the camera to place focus where you wish and then half press the shutter to lock focus there, recompose your picture and press the shutter. Although the latter sounds more clunky, I suspect that most will find it the quickest and most intuitive method. **Note:** you also have available a more specialized focus area in Face and Face Eye Priority. Turn this on and, as the name implies, it will find a face in the picture and focus on that automatically. You will see a green frame around the face when this is working. If you set **Face & Eye Priority** the camera will not only focus on a face but if it can detect the subject's eye it will focus on that.

## The AutoFocus Mode

**AF Area**, above, tells the E-M10 MkIII where it should focus. **AutoFocus Mode** tells it the type of autofocusing. **S-AF**, single autofocus, will focus once when you press/ half press the shutter button and not focus again until you press/ half press the shutter again. That works for static or slow moving subjects and is the base method. **C-AF**, continuous autofocus is intended for moving subjects. When you press/ half press the shutter button the camera focuses. However, all the time you keep the shutter half pressed the E-M10 MkIII will retain focus on the subject. So even if the subject is moving towards you, the camera keeps focus on them without any intervention on your part. Obviously, this cannot be foolproof, especially with a randomly moving subject like a football player but the camera does try to predict where they will be and it can work surprisingly well. You can use **S-AF** on quickly moving subjects but the problem is that between the time the camera has focused and the shutter firing, the subject will have moved enough to render them out of focus. **MF**, manual focus, needs practice but is handy because focus is put precisely where you want it by your own hand. It can be especially useful for movie shooting because the 'hunting' for focus that can occur when the subject changes position looks particularly unpleasant. **S-AF+MF** does what it says, it keeps the lens focusing ring active during autofocusing (it normally disables it) so that after the camera has focused, you can tweak it if you wish. **C-AF+TR** add **TR**acking to the C-AF. a small square looking something like a gunsight appears on the monitor. If you touch the subject on screen, the focus locks onto the subject and attempts to track it wherever it goes. If you touch on something in the centre of the screen and then turn the camera left or right, even though the object is now on the extreme side of the screen the gunsight box will still be on it and maintaining focus. It would be tempting to use this method all the time but the computing load it puts on the camera's processor is too much for it to be a reliable one stop solution. Also, anything coming between the focused object and camera can lead it to lose its lock. If lock is lost, the box turns red. **Note:** since stabilization takes a lot of computing power, when using **C-AF** or **TR** it can be a good idea to switch it off to free up some processing cycles.

## Shutter

The E-M10 MkIII has 3 shutter settings, **Mechanical**, **Anti-Shock** and **Silent**. The latter must be explicitly set in the **AP** mode. It is fully electronic, that is to say it works by an electronic readout of the sensor only, not using the metal blinds of the mechanical shutter at all. It has limitations on the E-M10 MkIII in that you can't use flash with it and the low focus light is disabled. There is also a danger of a type of motion distortion known as the jello effect if it is used on moving subjects.

✱ The **Mechanical Shutter** is the basic one. You have shutter speeds up to 1/4000th and the flash can be used at up to 1/250th. The one downside of the mechanical shutter is a possibility of shutter shock. This is a phenomenon which can occur at shutter speeds between roughly 1/60th and 1/400th. It is caused by the fast, sudden deceleration of the shutter blind as it reaches the end of its travel. It manifests itself as a slight blurring of the image. It does not always occur and can often only be detected at high image magnifications. Nonetheless, the possibility can be eliminated by the use of the

✱ **Anti-Shock** shutter. It is denoted by a black diamond beside the shutter icon. This is a hybrid of the mechanical and electronic shutters, where exposure is started with the electronic shutter but finished with the mechanical one. It allows for use of the flash and low light focusing lamp and shutter speeds down to 60 seconds. It is phased out above around 1/400th and the fully mechanical shutter takes over. There's no reason not to use this all the time

✱ **Sequential Shooting** comes in two forms, **High** and **Low**. **High** shoots at nearly 9 frames per second, **Low** at just under 5fps. Apart from the speed, the main difference between them is that at the **High** setting the focus point and exposure are set at the first frame taken on starting the sequence. If, during the sequence the subject moves out of focus, the pictures will be out of focus. Ditto the exposure, if during the sequence the subject moves into the shade, your picture will be under-exposed. With **Low** focus and exposure is adjusted for every frame shot. That's why it can't be as fast, of course. For most sports, five frames or so per second is ample

## <u>Highlight</u>

this control is known as Curves in Photoshop and other image processing programs. Essentially it brightens highlights, midtones or shadows independently of one another, so giving much more control than the more usual Contrast which affects the entire image. Below I show the normal linear setting next to the maximum contrast setting. I regularly use **Highlight** to tweak the white backing paper I use in product shots for my YouTube videos. A boost to the highlights with the

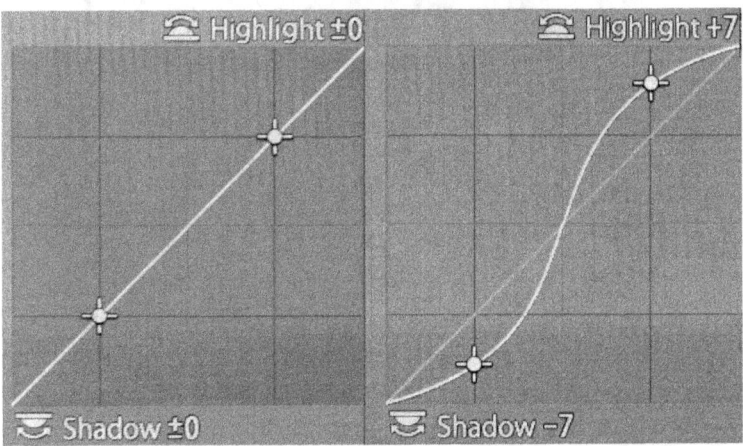

front dial is very useful to make sure the paper looks pristine white on the final image.

## Top Controls

The majority of control over a complex, dedicated imaging computer, which is what the Olympus E-M10 MkIII really is, is via the 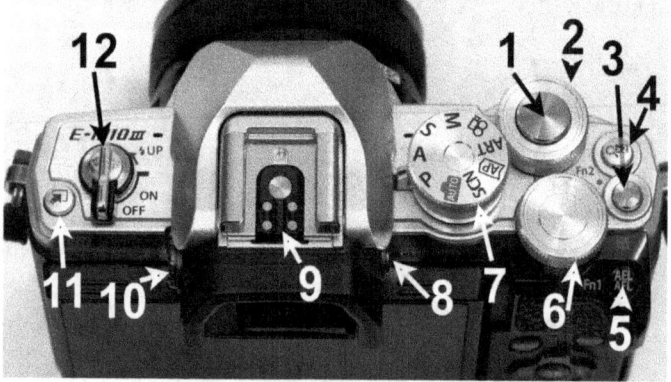 button. There are a few things so basic that they must be controlled by exterior levers and buttons. Those controls do not differ greatly from the ones which film camera users from the previous century would have been familiar. Set the camera to **M** anual on the **Mode** dial and you can control shutter speed and aperture directly. Change the **ISO** button and you have changed the 'film' speed. The rest of the external controls are essentially shortcuts to often used menu items. Here is a brief rundown on the basics of the body controls of the E-M10 MkIII.

1.The **Shutter Release** button. No need to emphasize the importance of this! It performs more than one function, though. A half press on it will set the exposure and focus point while in **Sequence** mode it will keep the shutter firing at high speed as long as you hold it down. Its exact functionality can be set in **Custom A→AEL/AFL**

2.The **Front Dial** It has the same multi-faceted role in the control of the E-M10 MkIII as the **Rear Dial (4)** being used for anything from selecting and altering settings on the **Super Control Panel** (I'll call it **SCP** for brevity from now on) to basics like shutter speed and aperture. It is a fair assumption that if it would feel natural to alter something with the dials, Olympus will have implemented it. **Note:** you can swap some functions between the front and rear dials in **Custom B→Dial Function**

3.The **Movie** button. Press this at any time and the camera will start shooting a video using the default settings you have made in **Video→Video Frame Rate & Video Bit Rate**

4.The **Fn2** button by default brings brings a Digital Tele-converter into play. It really does no more than crop the image and then upsample it to size again with the attendant loss of sharpness of such an operation. In these days of cheap zoom lenses it is hardly necessary and does no more than you can do yourself by a simple crop of the image. I find a far more practical use of **Fn2** is Magnify. This enlarges the view of the image making precise focusing very easy

5.The **Fn1** button. It can be assigned various functions but by default and as marked, it will lock Focus or exposure and I think most would find this the most useful function.

6. The **Rear Dial - see (2) Front Dial**

7. The **Mode Dial**. This is the arguably the most important control on the camera so I have dealt with it specifically on the **Mode Dial** page **Note:** when using the **A** and **S** modes, the front dial will be default alter the exposure compensation

8. The **Monitor** button. This controls the whether the image is on the EVF or the Monitor or shifted automatically. The 2 screens are the biggest user of battery power on any digital camera so it would not make sense to have them active at the same time. For that reason the EVF senses when it is not being used and transfers the view to the monitor and vice versa. If you press and hold the **Monitor** button you can choose between setting it explicitly to EVF or Monitor or to switch between them automatically. The sensor used to trigger the switch is on the top right of the eyecup and operates when your eye (or hand!) is within 5cm of it. **Note:** when you tilt the monitor, it automatically switches viewing to itself and keeps it there

9. The **Hot Shoe** for mounting a flash gun. Olympus's supplied FL-LM3 flash is small and convenient but obviously lacks power for the meatier tasks. Any flash from Metz, Nissin or Olympus and Panasonic themselves made to the Micro Four Thirds standard will work perfectly in **TTL** mode, removing any need for working out aperture settings and conserving battery power at the same time. The FL-LM3 can be used to trigger off-camera flash(es) for wireless operation

10. The **EVF** (electronic view finder) **diopter adjustment**. To find the sharpest position to suit your eyesight, bring up a screen of information via the

**INFO** button and turn the adjustment until it looks its clearest

11.The **Shortcut** button. Whichever **Mode** you are in, this button brings up on the monitor a relevant set of adjustments. Perhaps the most useful to experienced photographers is the **S**uper **C**ontrol**P**anel evoked when the camera is in **P A S** or **M** modes. It puts on one screen every parameter that you are likely to need while taking pictures. Use the **Rear Dial** to select a parameter, the **Front Dial** to change it. Or tap it with your finger once to select it, or twice to bring it up ready for altering via the **Front Dial**

12.The **On/Off** switch. Pretty straightforward. **Note:** if you find the switch **On** but the camera is dead, it has probably turned itself off after being idle for 4 hours. Switching **Off** and then **On** brings your E-M10 MkIII back to life. A push beyond **Off** springs up the very handy built in flash

## Mode Dial

The **Mode** dial is one of the most important controls on the camera. Most photographers use the **A** or **S** mode as their basic setting because while automating the exposure, at the same time they allow control over how your picture will look.

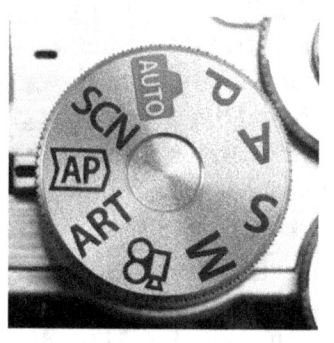

### Auto

the simplest setting. Set to this, the E-M10 MkIII becomes a point and shoot, albeit of exceptionally high quality.

In this mode, if you press the **Info** button a tab appears on the right of the monitor. Touch this and you can control **Color Saturation** (intensity of the colours), **Color Image** (the overall tint of the image), the **Brightness** of the image (light or dark), **Blur Background** (this changes the aperture of the lens, gaining more blur by using a faster shutter speed and wider lens aperture, **Express Motions** prevent or make blur on a moving subject (this changes the shutter speed, faster for sharp moving images, slower for blurry ones), an artistic effect but a bit hit and miss until you get used to it. There is also the **Shooting Tips** section wherein lies good advice on how to get better pictures from Olympus.

### P(program)

the camera chooses the shutter speed and aperture. It will find what it considers the optimum balance between **A**perture and **S**hutter speed. While you can use a fixed **ISO** it makes most sense to give the camera maximum flexibility by setting it to **Auto ISO**

## A (aperture Priority

You set the aperture, the camera varies the shutter speed to suit your setting. Aperture is the deciding factor in how much depth of field you have in your picture. For a portrait, you would probably want any distracting background elements to be blurred, in order to focus attention on your subject. For that you would limit your depth of field (obtain shallow depth of field) by using a wide aperture, that is opening your lens to its maximum f/3.5 or f/2.8, f/2 or f/1.4 if you have it. By stopping down to f/8 or lower you gain wide depth of field so that you can get more of your picture in focus. If you are photographing a field of flowers, you can get flowers from near to far in focus. The downside to a small aperture is that to maintain the correct exposure, the shutter speed must be lower. This can lead to blurring of the image due to the camera moving during the exposure. Or, if there is anything moving in your picture, motion blurring.

## S (Shutter Priority)

If you are photographing your children running around, they can move a surprisingly long way in, say 1/60th of a second. With **S** you can set a shutter speed to avoid the picture-spoiling motion blur that a slow shutter speed would entail. The downside of a high shutter speed is that the lens aperture must be wider to bring in enough light for correct exposure. That, as I previously said, cuts your depth of field, making your focusing very critical, just what you don't want for a child's unpredictable movement. What the shutter speed gives, the aperture takes away and vice versa. As with politics, exposure is the art of compromise.

## M(Manual)

leaves you to set both shutter speed and aperture. It can't achieve anything that **A** or **S** don't but some people prefer to 'do it all'. **Note:** in all of the previous, I have not mentioned the effect of the **ISO** setting. If you up the **ISO** setting you can have greater depth of field combined with higher shutter speeds. It looks like a win/win situation. Unfortunately, as with everyday life, there are very few win/ win scenarios. As you raise the **ISO** setting, you are not increasing the amount of light, you are merely amplifying what you have. And as with a radio with a poor signal, the more you turn it up, the more background noise there is. On an imaging sensor, it manifests itself as a random 'rash' on your picture. This juggling act between shutter speed, aperture and ISO is at the heart of photography - only you can decide where your compromise will be. **Note:** a handy use of **M** is to set the shutter speed and aperture you want and then set the **ISO** to **Auto**. It can't brighten the ambient light, though, so ultimately, handy or not, it is one more compromise.

## M(Movie)

gives you direct access to the **Movie** options when you press the **Shortcut** button. **Standard** (1080p) is the most versatile and currently the standard for YouTube and other video sites. On the E-M10 MkIII it is also the setting which gives you access to various creative effects with a press on the **Info** button. **4K** shoots large videos, 3840x2160 pixels with correspondingly large file sizes. You need a fast SD card to record them, UHS 3 will do the trick. Don't let a slower card stop you trying 4k, though. It rarely approaches a card's maximum speed. While **4k** monitors and TVs are not yet mainstream shooting in 4k could future proof your videos but at a cost of much greater file sizes and thus storage requirements. I find the main reason for shooting **4k** is the ability to crop, zoom and pan around your video in post processing before saving it as a 1080p (1920x1080)movie. **Clips** are handy little snippets of video which are preset to 1,2,4 or 8 seconds (with more added up to 16 seconds total if you press the **Rec** button while recording). **Note:** a good use of **Clips** is when you might want to shoot a quick snatch of video while shooting stills. Say you are with your family on a beach and shooting pictures as the children play in the waves. The camera is set to **Aperture** mode, 4:3 aspect ratio. If you now set the **Mode** dial to Movie, you can continue shooting stills with the those settings. Suddenly, you see a bigger wave coming in that will splash them. Just press the **Rec** button and the camera will shoot a **Clip**. You can then go back to shooting stills as before but the camera is remains ready for a short video. **H**igh **S**peed shoots 1280x720 (**HD**) video at 120 frames per second. Played back at 30fps, that slows movement down by a factor of four, 5 seconds shooting becoming 20 seconds of playback. It's a familiar effect these days but still an intriguing one. The **Effects** show when you press the **Shortcut** button and are pretty straightforward, if a bit cheesy. The Movie Tele-converter, far right, just crops the image and blows it up with attendant loss of quality. It's no substitute for a proper telephoto or zoom lens. It's versatile though, in that you can move the magnified area around on screen and with the left hand icon turn it on and off while shooting.

## ART

mode gives you access to 15 filters plus variations on them. The **Shortcut** button brings them up along the bottom of the screen and their effect is applied as you go through them using the front or rear dials. Using the up and down arrows, you can access some effects to add to the filter, so if you are using the **Watercolor filter you can decorate it with a frame or soft focus effect, for example. Just press** Shortcut to bring up the **Art** menu and then press the up or down arrow to access the effects. My favourite here is **Partial Color** and the E-M10 MkIII has the easiest implementation of it I have seen.

## AP

mode is for the advanced facilities of the Olympus E-M10 MkIII.

### Live Comp

(needs the camera on a tripod) lets you make a basic exposure and then only registers changes which are brighter than the original exposure. Let's say you are photographing the outside of your house at night. Press the shutter button and the camera will make a basic exposure taking into account the lit windows, any street lighting etc. Now take a narrow beam torch and trace around the door with it. The monitor will show you the house with the door outlined by your torch. Do this for other features and they will show up outlined as well. There are endless creative possibilities here. Excellent for start trails too. The camera makes a base exposure for any trees or buildings in the foreground but as the stars above move across the sky, being brighter than the black sky, the camera records them as they go. It'll take some experimentation to get it perfect but what a wonderful way to spend an hour or two.

### Live Time

(tripod again) is used for making long exposures and showing you the results as you go along. At its simplest, for a night shot press the shutter button and watch the monitor as the exposure builds up. When the night shot has built up enough exposure to show the brightness and detail you want, press the shutter button to stop the exposure.

### Multiple Exposure

with this set you will see a Multiple Exposure icon bottom left of the monitor. Take your first picture. Wait a moment and line up your second picture. You will see the first picture overlaid on it. When it is how you want, take the second picture and the camera will combine them.

### HDR

(**H**igh **D**ynamic **R**ange. if you take a picture of scene with an extreme tonal range, the camera's sensor cannot encompass them all. An example would be a picture of a room interior with a small window with a view out onto a garden. A good indoor exposure for the room, the furniture, paintings on the wall etc might be ISO 200 1/25th at f/4. The garden outside might require ISO 200 1/4000th at f/4. A room exposure renders the window a white detail-less rectangle. An exposure for the garden outside renders the interior an inky black. A compromise exposure of 1/250th at f/4 renders nothing satisfactorily. **HDR** takes a series of exposures and combines them, attempting to show detail both in the room and outside the window. It can be very effective but can also lead to rather flat looking results. **HDR2** is a stronger version of the basic effect. **HDR** works by taking a series of images at different exposures and combining them so is best done on a tripod.

### Silent Mode

uses an electronic rather than the mechanical shutter. This shutter, the same one used when shooting video, is silent. Very useful at a christening, say where you could take pictures without the giveaway clack of a mechanical shutter. The focus confirmation beep and the focusing aid light are turned off and you cannot use flash. With **Silent Shutter** enabled, if you press the down arrow you can select **Sequential** (burst) and timer modes using it. **Note:** be cautious using the electronic shutter on quickly moving subjects as it can lead to a form of distortion which leads uprights to appear slanting. It is called the jello effect and endemic to all electronic shutters to some degree.

### Panorama

simply superimposes guides on the monitor to indicate how far to turn the camera to get adequate overlap on each frame for a satisfactory stitching process. The camera, disappointingly, doesn't do the stitching automatically and you must do it in post processing. Before starting your panorama, press an arrow key to indicate to the camera your direction of panning. You can take up to 10 frames for your panorama, if you need fewer, just press **OK** to halt the process. I find it best to shoot with the camera in portrait orientation for panoramas to get adequate height to the shot. Otherwise it is rather too long and thin.

### Keystone compensation

when you photograph a building, especially a tall one, you need to tilt the camera upwards to get the whole building in the frame. This leads to the sides of the building appearing to converge and looks unnatural, as if it is toppling over backwards. It actually does happen to the image projected onto the retina by your eye as well but your brain, knowing the top of the building is the same width as the bottom, corrects for it without any conscious intervention. Turning the front or rear dials lets you compensate for the effect in camera.

## *AE BKT*

Auto-exposure bracket - sometimes a large area of light sky you might get on a seascape or an unusual light foreground, a snow covered ski slope for example, might lead the camera to misjudge the exposure and render an image too light or too dark. It can sometimes be difficult to know what the correct exposure would be so **AE BKT** shoots 3 frames 1 stop apart or 5 frames 0.7 stops apart. This allows you to choose the best exposure afterwards. It would be very rare for the camera to misjudge an exposure, even a difficult one, by as much as one stop.

## *Focus BKT*

are making a landscape photograph with something prominent in the foreground, it can be difficult to know where to focus. **Focus BKT** shoots 7 pictures while focusing from foreground to background of your subject. You can then choose the best focusing compromise from among them. It has two settings, one with a smaller, one with a larger distance between focus points. **Note:** you can combine these images into an image with a very wide depth of field on post processing with suitable software. Results can be unpredictable so some trial and error will be required. You will see some of the finest results from this technique in the work of photographers taking close-ups or macro shots of insects.

## SCN

opens up 6 panels covering broad areas of photography. After picking a suitable one there are various more detailed aspects to choose from along the bottom of the screen. All of them can be achieved in more hands on modes like **A** or **S** but it's useful to have these presets as a down and dirty quick fix. The downside is that they don't allow for any manual input so you won't learn much from using them.

# Rear Controls

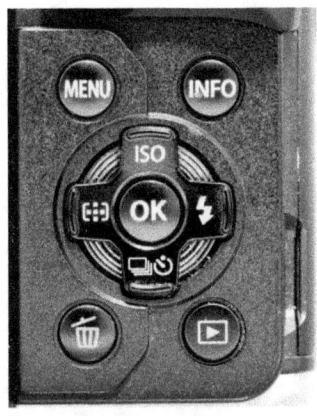

The **Menu** button. As you'd expect it accesses the menu. When you are in the menu, it serves to step backwards through it The **INFO** button. This switches between screens showing image only, shooting information, histogram and/or level gauge depending on the settings in **Custom→C1→LV-Info**. It performs a similar function in **Playback Note:** If you press and hold the **INFO** button you can scroll through the screens using the front or rear dials if you prefer

The **Arrow Pad** During normal shooting it gives direct access to the **ISO, Flash, Shutter Mode** and **AF Area** settings. After pressing one of the Arrows, the Arrow keys then become a means of moving through the options available (you can use the front or rear dials also)

The **OK** button. Apart from the obvious confirmation of menu items and dialog boxes, in **P A S M** modes it brings up the either the SCP or the **Live Control**. Since the **Shortcut** button brings up the **SCP** the OK button is better set to the **Live Control**

The **Playback** button. It accesses the images stored on the camera for review

The **Erase button**. In the unlikely event that anyone takes a less than perfect picture on the E-M10 MkIII, bring it up in **Playback** mode and press this to dispense with the offending image. **Note:** if you want to erase more than one image, touch the screen to bring up the row of icons at the bottom. Touch icon to bring up the grid view. You are will see - Touch that and it changes to . Now, when you touch an image in the grid it will show a tick. When you've selected all you want, press and you're done

# Shooting Menu 1

## Reset

The obvious use for **Reset** is if you are selling the camera. However, it is possible with digital cameras to alter so many settings that you can't remember what you have done. In this case, a **Reset** will always take you back to a known point. Unless you are selling the camera, probably best to use a **Basic Reset** first with a **Full** if that doesn't resolve the problem. Both settings leave **Date** and **Time** settings intact.

### *Full*

This resets more or less everything. For example, if you have adjusted the EVF brightness and colour to your taste, they will be set back to their default. Essentially, **Full** puts the camera back to the settings as they were it came out of the box.

### *Basic*

Use this if you have made an alteration to a setting and don't remember what you did. It will set things like the **Picture Mode** back to its **Natural** default but leave personal settings like your EVF settings alone.

## Picture Mode

The comprehensive list of **Picture Modes** is mostly self-explanatory. There are some highly sophisticated effect here all of which are shown in real time on the monitor. You can view them in the EVF, too. When choosing an effect, a press on the right cursor button will bring up a selection of parameters which can be altered to taste. Depending on the effect chosen, these will affect sharpness, contrast, brightness and so on. Some effects allow you to add one effect to another or change the nature of the chosen effect. Mono, for example, gives you a choice of colour filter emulations, red to darken the sky for example but also to blue tone the subject and even make it high or low key. A highly popular effect is the **Partial Color** which enables you to shoot black and white pictures but with one colour retained. Photographing a blue eyed person, for example, you could highlight their blue eyes by making them the only colour element in the picture. It is a haunting effect with many uses but a little more complicated to use than others. Having set the **Picture Mode** to **Partial Color**, you'll need to turn the **Mode Dial** to **Art**. Press **OK** and choose from the three levels of **Partial Color** available. Press **OK** again and the **Color Ring** comes up. Turn the front or rear dial to select the desired colour and intensity of colour you wish to retain. There are three levels of **Partial Color**, available, 1 being the least selective and 3 the most. **Note:** Modes cannot be applied to **RAW** files. If you shoot RAW+JPG, only the **JPG** will have the mode applied. Some of the Modes impose heavy processing overhead so may not work in video shooting and may lead to jerky viewing image in stills. Any blurring or jerkiness you see will not be present in the picture you take.

## Digital Tele-Converter

This works by cropping the centre portion of the sensor and then sampling it back up to the 4608x3456 pixels, giving the effect of doubling the focal length of the lens. In doing this sharpness is lost, naturally, since you are using only a cropped central portion of the sensor for your image. Keep in mind that if your usage for the picture is on a tablet, FHD monitor or high quality print of 10 inches across, say, you would be better simply to crop the image in post processing. Since there is no need to up-sample in this case, the intended use being smaller than the crop would be, there will be no quality loss from the original shot. In these days of cheap and sharp zoom lenses there is little need for a digital zoom. The **Digital Tele Converter** can be used in video but again I find the effect distinctly inferior to using a zoom to enlarge the image. One for emergencies only! **Note:** if set **On** while shooting **RAW** a white box will appear around the centre of the image to tell you where the crop would take place. However, the **Digital Tele-Converter** only works with **JPG** files and only those will be cropped and up-sampled.

## Metering

This is called **Digital ESP Metering** It measures a matrix of over 300 samples of the scene brightness and calculates the optimum exposure. It's the best all round choice and often the only one you will use. If the scene looks too dark or light, a touch of **Exposure Compensation** will take care of it but it's usually not necessary. If you set Face Priority focusing, metering knows that and exposes with that in mind

This meters the centre of the subject and the background separately and averages them. It assumes that the most important element of your picture is in the centre and weights the exposure to that. It's a method that was used by pre-digital cameras and is superseded by the much more accurate and consistent matrix metering above

Spot metering, this meters a tiny central point of the scene. The metering area is indicated by a thin circular overlay on the screen. It is of use where your subject is a small object set against a background of a radically different brightness. For example, if you photograph a crow standing in a snow covered field, the camera's exposure system cannot know that it is only the crow that you're concerned about photographing. It will try to average out the exposure, albeit intelligently, and the crow will almost certainly be under-exposed. Set Spot Metering and line the circle up with the bird and exposure will be made entirely for the bird. This is not perfect, however, because of the way that exposure metering works. It assumes that any subject will have an overall average light reflectance of 18%. While that is true of many scenes, it is not true of a crow which, being jet black, probably reflects no more than 2% of the light that falls on it. The meter will therefore expose to make the crow look a mid grey - in other words over expose it! Spot metering is very useful on occasion but must be used intelligently

**HI**light tells the meter that your subject is light and it exposes accordingly

**SH**adow tells the meter that your subject is dark and so it exposes to preserve the dark nature of the subject. The crow would be an example
**Note:** I don't use all these Metering settings much. Generally, I find it easier to use **Digital ESP Metering** and use **Exposure Compensation** to get the exposure how I want it.

# Shooting Menu 2

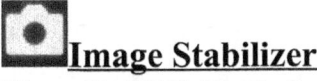

## Image Stabilizer

The stills **IBIS** (**In B**ody **I**mage Stabilization) of the E-M10 Mark lll is highly effective. The rule of thumb formula for the shutter speed necessary for a given lens with 35mm film cameras was that it should match the lens. Thus, a 50mm lens would need a minimum shutter speed of 1/50th to get sharp, blur free results. Micro Four Thirds cameras with their smaller sensor halve the angle of view of any given lens, effectively doubling the magnification, so a 50mm lens needs 50x2, a minimum shutter speed of 1/100th. A 25mm lens would need 1/50th and so on. With the stabilization on this camera you can hand hold a 25mm lens reliably at 1/10th, even 1/5th depending on your hands!

**Note:** These settings apply to stills only. You set the stabilization for video in the **Movie** menu.

## AF Illuminator

The camera will focus reliably and quickly in remarkably dim light but there is a limit. When that limit is reached, with **AF Illuminator** set **On** the camera sends out a beam of light to assist the system. It's best to leave this **On** unless you are using the camera stealthily, at a wedding, for example where you don't want to disturb the proceedings

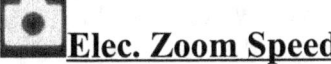

## Elec. Zoom Speed

If you have a power zoom like the Olympus 12-50mm, this sets the speed at which power zooming takes place. The power zoom is mainly useful for video, since it zooms at a consistent speed, something hard to do manually.

## 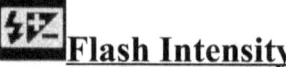Flash Intensity

This somewhat cryptic image means flash intensity adjustment. The E-M10 MkIII's built in flash determines its exposure by sending out a pre-flash and measuring and averaging the light that comes back. Then, having determined the exposure, it fires a full strength pulse of the required intensity. Though generally accurate, a light skinned person wearing dark clothing can cause over-exposure of the face because while the overall scene may be dark and require more flash light than average,the face does not. The converse applies with a dark skinned person in light coloured clothing. The clothing requires less exposure than average which will lead to the face being too dark. This camera setting can correct that. The +3 and -3 range available is generous. The E-M10's metering will very rarely require more than a + or -1 adjustment. **Note:** if you are using an Olympus accessory flash triggered by the camera's flash and have the accessory flash set to **Manual** this setting will have no effect. If you are using the Olympus accessory flash on TTL (Through The Lens) control, both the camera flash and external flash will be affected.

## Intrvl. Sh./Time Lapse

The Olympus E-M10 MkIII can take pictures at set intervals automatically and, if you wish, assemble them into a **Time Lapse** movie.

***Number of Frames***

Shoot from one to 999 frames.

## *Start Waiting Time*

Sets a time to wait from before starting the interval shooting. If you wanted to make a dawn to dusk Time Lapse movie of your home showing how the daylight quality and direction changes you would want to start it at dawn. If it is summer and sunrise is at 5am you might not want to get up press the shutter button. So, before going to bed at 11pm, set the **Start Waiting Time** to 6 hours and let the Olympus wake itself up and start shooting for you.

## *Interval Length*

The time from the end of one exposure to the start of another.

## *Time Lapse Movie*

With this **Off**, you will simply record images as set previously. If you want to make a **Time Lapse** movie from them, you will need to do it in your editing software in post processing. With it set **On** the camera will automatically compile the movie to the standards set in **Movie Settings** below. **Note:** When the camera compiles the frames into a **Time Lapse** movie, it does not delete the separate frames that make it up. So, if you shoot 100 frames, you will have 101 items on your SD card, 100 stills and the compiled movie. After your **Time Lapse** is completed, the camera reverts to normal shooting. If you want to shoot another **Time Lapse** you must set it **On** again. Also, the **Time Lapse** movie will be in whatever aspect ratio you have set. If you go straight to it from 4:3 stills shooting the movie will be in 4:3 ratio. Since practically all video for YouTube etc is shot at 16:9 you will need to explicitly set it before starting to shoot.

## *Movie Setting*

You have a choice of **Movie Resolutions** and **Frame Rates**. Assuming you want the standard 16:p aspect ratio the **Resolution** choices are

**HD** - 1280x720 pixels. This is rather low resolution and quality by modern standards. It is, however, the only one that allows the 30fps **Frame Rate** necessary for smooth playback

**FHD** - 1920x1080 pixels. The standard for most video nowadays. The highest **Frame Rate** allowed is 15fps which is a bit choppy but can be acceptable for scenes without any sudden movement

**4k** - 3840x2160 pixels. Very high quality but not many monitors or TVs have such a high resolution yet. Maximum **Frame Rate** is 5fps which is more like a rapid slideshow than a **Time Lapse**. It eats disk space, too

**Note:** bear in mind that you do not have to make the **Time Lapse** movie in camera. For decent quality,**FHD** at 25 or 30fps is ideal. Most video software will do this easily. The formula for working out **Time Lapse** movies is the desired Duration for movie = Duration in seconds x Frame Rate so if you want a 30 second movie using 30fps, you need to shoot 30x30 or 900 frames. If you want a one minute long movie at 15 fps covering a 12 hour span, you need need Time Span To Cover (in seconds)/ (Length of Movie desired x Frames Per Second). So, for a one minute movie at 15fps you will need 60s x 15 = 900 frames. There are 12x60x60 = 43200 seconds in 12 hours, so you will need to fire one frame every 43200/900 seconds = an interval of 48 seconds.

## ⚡ RC Mode

This stands for **R**emote **C**ontrol and is useful if you have an Olympus (or other Micro Four Thirds compatible) accessory flash which can operate in **Slave Mode**. With **RC Mode Mode** on, the E-M10's built in flash will act as a controller for it. This is known as **Master** mode and not only will the built in flash trigger the accessory flash but it will tell it how much flashlight to deliver for a good exposure. The built in flash on any camera is a little crude in terms of lighting quality. Its use is mainly to provide some light when there isn't enough naturally, as is often the case at a social gathering, for example. An accessory flash held a out at arms length above and to the right or left of the subject will provide much more interesting, even artistic lighting. With **RC Mode**, you can place the flash wherever you wish and have the camera take care of the exposure. It's a very useful feature and one which many more expensive cameras do not sport.

# Video Menu

## Movie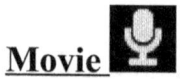

This gives you the option of recording sound with your video or not. If you are going to add your own voiceover sound can be a nuisance as when a police car passes with its siren going. Other times you may want the voices of your children on the video. This setting gives you the choice plus another useful one, the facility to cut down on wind noise, a blustering, rumbling sound that can ruin a video. If you want the ambient sound of waves breaking or the wind rustling the leaves in the tree or even if you are videoing someone speaking or singing out of doors, wind noise reduction will keep the rumbling to a minimum. It's not perfect but it helps. Best not to keep it on all the time since it does detract from overall sound quality a little.

## Recording Volume

For normal sound levels you can leave this at the default mid setting. An ideal setting is when the meter reaches the marked -12dB on the loudest sounds. Since 'clipping', when a sound overloads the microphone, sounds highly unpleasant it is best to err on the lower side of the meter. Even the loudest transient sounds should never go above the 0dB mark and into the red. If you making a video of a very loud rock band, you'll probably need to set the meter right down to -10dB. A change of 3dB represents a doubling of the sound intensity, while a change if 1dB is about the smallest change the human ear can appreciate.

## AF Mode

**S-AF**(single autofocus) - Half press the shutter button to focus then press the **Rec Button** to start and stop video recording. A half press of the shutter button while shooting will re-focus. This isn't ideal because the focusing is very sudden which looks awful in video. Best used on subjects where, once focused they will not move very much

**C-AF**(continuous autofocus) - the camera will focus automatically all the time. If the camera mis-focuses, a half press on the shutter button at any time will shift focus to your chosen point

**MF** (manual focus) - is the professional's choice because you can control the exact speed of focus and the exact focusing point. **Focus Peaking** is an enormous help here. **MF** is very difficult on moving subjects

**S-AF+MF**- allows you to modify the camera's focus point by making the lens focusing ring active so that you can override the camera at any time. Handy for situations where you have limited depth of field and the camera focus spot is not precise enough

**C-AF+TR** (tracking) - allows you to pick a focus point which the camera will track and attempt to keep in focus. A half press on the shutter button brings up a green box. Line this up with whatever you want to keep in focus and start the video with whichever button you have set to do so. You can also touch the monitor and the tracking focus point will move to track the subject you have picked on screen

## Image Stabilizer

Use **Off** when the camera is on a tripod or otherwise securely held steady. **M-IS 1** uses the excellent sensor stabilization combined with digital stabilization. This crops the image a little. It is especially useful for steadying walking shots where you are holding the camera out in front of you. **M-IS 2** is the sensor stabilization alone and the best all round choice. Olympus are rightly famous for their stabilization system.

## Elec. Zoom Speed

If you have a power zoom like the Olympus 12-50mm, this sets the speed at which power zooming takes place. Useful if you have the 12-50mm Olympus zoom. Power zooming is especially useful in video because it is able to zoom at a steady speed, almost impossible manually.

## Video Frame Rate

The basic choice is 30fps or 25fps. As a rule of thumb, 30fps is used in the USA and 25fps in Europe. The difference was due to the different TV standards in the two areas. These days it hardly matters and both rates will play back happily on any TV or screen anywhere. If you are shooting for YouTube or other online outlets, they will happily accept either. 24fps is an odd one. It exists because film cameras from past shot at 24fps and some enthusiasts maintain that it gives a more filmic look to their work. I cannot see it myself and so mainly use 25fps.

## Video Bit Rate

The higher the bit rate the better the quality but the bigger the file. **Note:** the choices of movie size and quality are governed by **Video Frame Rate** and **Video Bit Rate** but all the possibilities are not seen in the menu system. Neither are they easily available with the **Mode** Dial set to Movie. This is my suggested way of setting the movie quality you require. I find it best to decide what quality I want and stick to that for everything. My choice is for good general purpose use.

Set the Mode Dial to Movie

Set the video frame rate to 25 or 30fps as you wish

Set the video bit rate to Fine

Press the Shortcut button and choose Standard from the menu that appears at the bottom of the monitor

Set the Mode Dial to A

Press the Shortcut button and the SCP appears

Touch the Movie Setting panel to highlight it

Turn the front dial to set FHD F 25 or 30p

Now, whenever you press the Record button or the Mode Dial is set to Movie, that is the format you will shoot in. **Note:** 50 or 60 fps settings are best left to experts with the software and knowledge to handle them. If you find your file sizes are too large set the Video Bit Rate in step 3 to Normal

## Playback Menu

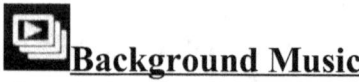

### **Background Music**

***Start***

Press OK with this highlighted and the slide show commences.

***BGM***

After some research, I surmise this stands for **B**ack**G**round **M**usic. You can download some from the Olympus web site if you must. My personal choice of music from the range offered is Off but John Cage's 4'33" of Silence is a reasonable substitute.

***Slide***

You can set this to make your slideshow encompass both videos and stills, just stills or just videos.

***Slide Interval***

The time between stills

***Movie Interval***

The time between Movies.

### **(Image Rotation)**

**Off**, if you are holding the camera in the landscape plane, you will need to turn it to view a picture shot in portrait orientation. This does mean that you see it at the full dimensions of the screen, however. If rotation is **On** a portrait image is displayed in the landscape plane with black bands either side. A portrait picture viewed in landscape plane will display considerably smaller but you avoid having to turn the camera.

### Edit

You can take a previously shot image on the SD card and make an edited copy of it. You do not lose the original.

### Sel. Image

Find the image you want to **Edit** and press **OK**. A menu appears.

### RAW Data Edit

If you have selected a **RAW** file to edit, a **JPG** copy is made for you to work on.

### JPG Data Edit

If you have selected a **JPG** file to edit, you are presented with a range of adjustments which are mainly self-explanatory. One that is not is **Shadow Adj** which tries to correct images shot against the light. For example, you make a Selfie with the sun behind you, so that your face is in shadow. **Shadow Adj** tries to correct for that. **e-Portrait** smooths out facial features and really ought to be a gimmick but is so well implemented that it isn't. If I ever find myself doing selfies, **e-Portrait** will be the first port of call after making the exposure. If you select a video file you can capture still images from it by using the arrow keys to find a frame and press **OK**. The image will be saved as a **JPG**. You can also **Trim** the movie and save it as a new file or replace the original with **Overwrite**. Olympus do like their cryptic icons. This

one enables you to crop the image. Use the front and rear dials to size the frame and the arrow keys to

place it. means you can reduce the image dimensions, handy for loading images to social media and sending by email.**Note:** if you select a **RAW** file to edit and select **Current** a **JPG** copy will be made with the setting currently in use. So, let's say you shoot a **RAW** file at 4:3 aspect ratio with **Auto White Balance**. If you them set the camera to 16:9 aspect ratio and fluorescent White Balance and then select

**Current**the **JPG** file will be trimmed to 16:9 and with fluorescent White Balance. If you choose **ART BKT JPG** copies are made using each of the art filters selected. Any editing on the image after that is carried out using the normal **JPG** editing.

*Image Overlay*

This only works with **RAW** files. After pressing this, select 2 or 3 files using the cursor keys and OK button. The camera will make a **JPG** file of the selected files overlaid on one another. It's hard to predict the results so if there is something in particular you want you will need to plan it carefully. If you want to combine more than 3 files, select the already overlaid file plus 2 others. You can do this as many times as you like. After the selecting the files to be overlaid, you will see the originals at the bottom of the monitor so that you can vary the brightness of each of them to get the effect you want. Press OK and the processing goes ahead.

## Print Order

If you have a suitable **DPOF** (Digital Print Order Format) printer you can connect the camera to it with the USB cable supplied and from **Print Order** select the images you wish to print. Or take the SD card into a print shop that supports **DPOF**.

*Select and Print Individually*

Press **OK** and find the image you wish to print. On the top right you can set the number of prints you want of the image. On pressing **OK** you are offered the choice of adding the **Date** and **Time** taken to be printed on the picture. You can repeat this for each image you want printed.

### *Print One Of Each Image*

As above but sets each image to have one print made.

## Reset Protect

When you press the **Playback** button to show the images stored on your SD Card there may be images you definitely do not wish to erase. If you press the

**OK** button you will see a key icon . Selecting this will protect your image from accidental erasure. You can unprotect an image by repeating this procedure. If you have many images protected it can get tedious, **Reset Protect** simply unprotects all protected images at once. **Note:** Pressing **Fn2** while an image is being displayed will also protect it and pressing again will unprotect it but this only works if the **Fn2** button is assigned a function other than its default **Magnify**.

## Connection to Smartphone

**Note:** before connecting for the first time, go to the **Setup Wi-Fi Settings** menu and check it is set to the default **Private** connection. It's also as well to Reset **Wi-Fi Settings** to be certain you are getting a clean start . You must have have Olympus's **Image Share** app installed on your phone. It is free for Android and Apple phones. The app allows you to control the Olympus E-M10 MkIII from your phone. It's best to download and install it before making the initial connection. To connect, follow the steps below.
**Highlight Connection to Smartphone and press OK**
A screen showing Preparing Wi-Fi Connection appears. Press **OK** again

A screen asking you to install the Olympus Image Share app appears. You will already have done this. Press **OK** again

You will see a messsage Wi-Fi starting, quickly followed by a page with a QR code on it

At the bottom of the Image Share opening page, beneath **Add Geotag** you will see a small camera and Wi-Fi Off logo. Touch that and **Easy Setup** appears

Touch that and the Easy Setup page appears. Press **Scan**

A rectangle appears on the smartphone screen. Line it up with the QR code on the camera

The smartphone confirms that the connection settings have been scanned - now press **Connect** at the bottom of the page

Press **Remote** at the top of the page. You will see the view from your camera on your smartphone

If you haven't seen it before, it's quite exciting, isn't it? **Note:** if for some reason you can't connect using the QR code, make sure that Wi-Fi is **On**. You can easily turn it on from the monitor, top left next to the battery state icon. Once it is on, go to your smartphone and tap connections where you'll see the E-M10 MkIII listed as on of the networks. Tap on it to connect and enter the eight digit password shown on the bottom of the monitor.

# Custom A. AF/MF

## AEL/AFL

This determines the function of the **AEL/AFL** button
(on top of the thumb grip) as it interacts with the
shutter button. It operates differently according to the
focus mode. To use it, frame the subject and press the
button. A green flag comes up on screen to indicate
that exposure or focus is locked. **Note:** this button is
also marked **Fn1** and can be assigned a different
function if you wish.

### S-AF

**Mode1** frame your scene. Exposure and focus are
locked by a half press of the shutter. All the time you
keep the shutter half pressed, exposure and focus
remain locked. This is the way most photographers
work. If you want exposure and focus for a person at
the edge of the frame, point the camera at them and
half press the shutter, thus setting focus and exposure.
All the time you keep the shutter half pressed, focus
and exposure will remain the same. Now reframe the
picture with your subject at the edge and press the
shutter. If at any time you press **AEL/AFL** button,
exposure will be locked at that point and a half press
on the shutter button will only change the focus
**Mode2** - When you half press the shutter, focus is set
but exposure is determined at the moment the shutter
fires. A press on the **AEL/AFL** again locks the
exposure while focusing is done as normal
**Mode3** - removes the focusing function from the
shutter button entirely. Exposure is set by half pressing
the shutter button but focusing only occurs when you
press the **AEL/AFL** button. Thus, once having pressed

the **AEL/AFL** button, focus remains set there until it is pressed again

For general purpose use, **Mode1** is the most intuitive for most photographers.

*C-AF*

**Mode1** half press sets the exposure and initiates focusing. Pressing the **AEL/AFL** locks the exposure but focusing continues unaffected

**Mode2** half pressing the shutter initiates **C-AF**. A full press sets the exposure and focus. Pressing the **AEL/AFL** button locks the exposure

**Mode3** half pressing the shutter sets the exposure, fully pressing then sets the focus. However, focusing only takes place while the **AEL/AFL** is pressed. This is the back button focusing favoured by sports and wildlife photographers. If you are using **AF-C** to keep focus on a player, when someone runs between him and the camera, it will try to refocus on the nearer blocking player. When your target player is in view again, the camera will have to start focusing all over again. The re-acquisition of focus that often the slowest part of **C-AF**. However, since the **AEL/AFL** is controlling focusing, if you stop pressing it when the view is blocked, it stops focusing at the moment you stop pressing. When your chosen player is visible gain, press the button to resume focusing where you left off

**Mode4** is the same as **Mode3** but exposure is set on actually taking the picture. I find this the most useful action mode since exposure is determined at the moment you take the picture

*MF*

**Mode1** a half press sets the exposure. Full press takes the picture. Pressing **AEL/AFL** locks the exposure

**Mode2** the exposure is set at the moment of taking the picture. **AEL/AFL** locks the exposure

**Mode3** this is a neat hybrid effect. You are set to manual focus but a press on the **AEL/AFL** button focuses the lens. Exposure is set by half pressing the shutter release. A handy way of quickly establishing a starting point for your own focusing. The Olympus E-M10 MkIII's focusing efficiency is such that you will find **MF** necessary only on rare occasions, mainly when you want pinpoint accuracy on an area of the image that is too small for the focusing area box

## AF Targeting Pad

While using the EVF you often need to move the **AF target frame**. You can use the arrow cursor keys but set this item **On** and you can use your finger on the monitor to shift it around. If you find yourself moving the area around by accident - your nose will be the culprit! - a double tap on the monitor will toggle it on and off. **Note:** if you have the **EVF Auto Switch** set **On** (Custom Menu H) you can only use the monitor for this when set flat against the camera. If you want to use it swung out from the camera, set **EVF Auto Switch** to **Off**. Then manually set the EVF on. Now the monitor will appear to be off but it will move the target frame where your finger sets it.

## Face Priority

Normally, the camera will focus on whatever is in the **AF Area** you have set. Setting **Face Priority** to **On** changes that so that the camera constantly searches the scene for a human face. When it finds one it encloses it in a white frame, sets focus on it and then tracks it, keeping it in focus even if you move the camera around. All the while correct focus is maintained, the frame turns green. Two flavours of **Face Priority** are

offered. Face Priority  itself just keeps the face in

focus. ![eye AF icon] focuses on the person's eye closest to the camera. **Note:** if you are using a sequential shutter setting, that is, shooting bursts of frames, the focus priority is set only for the first frame of the burst. After that it reverts to normal focusing.

## MF Assist

Good as the Olympus E-M10 MkIII's focusing system is, there are times when Manual Focusing is more appropriate. Video shooting is often better when manual focusing is used because it avoids the off-putting hunting backwards and forwards of focus that can occur when the image has low contrast or is in very low light. It is also necessary when using older lenses designed for film cameras hwich do not have an auto-focus system built in. Manual Focusing itself can be tricky, though so Olympus offers two methods of facilitating it.

### *Magnify*

Set **On**, when you turn the focusing ring on the lens, the centre portion of the image is magnified. Use the front or rear dials to vary the level of magnification. A touch on the shutter button will turn off the magnification to put you back into normal full frame view. Normally the centre portion of the image will be magnified but you can move the area with the arrow keys.

### *Peaking*

this outlines high contrast areas of the image in colour when you turn the lens focusing ring with the focused area being the most densely coloured. It is especially useful in that it gives you an idea of which parts of the image will be in focus along with the desired area. If you have 3 three faces in your pic and they are too far apart to all be in perfect focus, you can use the **Peaking** to get as even a distribution of colour among them as possible for the best compromise. **Note:** you can change the colour of the **Peaking** in Custom Menu C2. You can use **Magnify** and **Peaking** together if you wish.

## Reset Lens

This controls what happens to the lens focusing when you turn the camera on and off. With **Reset Lens Off** if you are focused at 1 metre when you turn the camera off, when turned on it will be focused at 1 metre still. Set **On**, when you switch on, the lens will always be focused at infinity. **Note:** if you change lenses while the camera is off, the focused position will not be reset and the lens will be at infinity regardless.

## Custom B. Button/Dial

### <u>Button Function</u>

This applies to the **Fn1** button marked **AFL/AEL**. In the default **AEL/AFL** mode its exact function is dictated by the setting in Custom Menu A **AEL/AFL**. To simplify it, in **Mode 1** and **Mode 2** of all focus mode settings, **S-AF**, **C-AF** and **MF**, when you press the **AEL/AFL** button,it locks the exposure. This can be useful when the scene you are focusing on has a very wide range of brightness. Say you are photographing a sunset with mountains in the foreground. The mountains will be much, much darker than the sky. If you framed the picture so that half was the sky and half the mountains, the camera cannot know that it is the sky, with its spectacular sunset that you want to show. Because half the scene is very dark, the camera will calculate an average exposure and the sky will be too light (ie overexposed). If you frame the scene so that most of the image is the sky and then press the **AEF/AEL** button, that will lock the exposure. You can now frame your picture as you wish and the sunset will be properly exposed. Don't leave it locked too long, though. Sunsets, especially in southern latitudes, lose brightness very quickly. The other settings are:

**S-AF Mode 3** - the camera focuses and then locks that focus position. So, if you focus on an object 1 metre away by pressing the button and then point the camera at something 20 metres away, focus will remain at 1 metre. **Note:** the focus stays where it was locked until you press the button again

**C-AF** - **Mode 3** and **Mode 4** - continuous autofocusing is started and continues while the button is pushed. Release the button and focusing stops
**MF** - **Mode 3**S-AF is performed. This is a hybrid of auto and manual focus, really. Press the button and the camera focuses but from that point on you must adjust the focus manually. You can press the button at any time to focus elsewhere
**Note:** when you set **AEL/AFL** in the **Custom A** menu, as you run though the options the effect of the **AEL/AFL** button is displayed below the main settings.

## Dial Function

this tailors the front and rear dials to your preference. The dials control **Exposure Compensation** and the main parameter of the **Mode** you have set. In Aperture **Mode**, for example you can have the rear dial control the aperture and the front dial the compensation or vice-versa. In **M Mode**, you can have the front dial control the aperture and the rear dial the shutter speed or vice-versa.

# Custom C1. Disp //PC

## Control settings

This sets what happens when you press the **OK** button while shooting. You can set it differently for each stills **Mode**, the choice being **LV-C** or LV-SCP. **LV** just means **live**. the **LV-C** option gives you quick access to overall shoot settings like **ISO** or Aspect Ratio that you might want to alter during a shoot. You can select a parameter from the right of the screen using the up/down arrow keys or the rear dial and alter it with the right/left arrow keys or the front dial **LV-SCP** is the **Super Control Panel**. It gives you access to a much wider range of options such as **Stabilization** on or off and the **AF Area** but is less quick to use. You can move around the screen using the rear dial or arrow pad or touching it if you prefer. Having highlighted a parameter, you can alter it with the rear dial, press OK or a double tap on it. **Note:** there's no point in setting the **SCP** in **P/A/S/M** because in all

those modes the 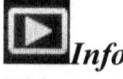 button accesses it directly anyway.

## /Info Settings

### *Info*

This setting controls what happens when you press the **INFO** while reviewing images. All unticked, the button does nothing. As you tick more boxes, a press on the **INFO** button when reviewing will step through them. They options are pretty straightforward. **Overall** gives you a histogram of the colour components of your image and the shooting information.

**Highlights and Shadow** gives you a flashing display
of which picture areas are clipped, that is do not
contain detail, being beyond the camera's ability to
capture them at the exposure used. **Light Box** gives
you a way to compare two images side by side. Get the
image you want on screen and press **Info** until a split
screen comes up. On the left will be a section of the
image you selected and on the right the next image
taken. Scroll through your images using the left and
right arrow keys or the front dial until you find the one
you want to compare. Turning the rear dial will
magnify both images.

*LV-Info*

This sets what you will see when you press the **Info**
button while shooting pictures. All boxes unticked
toggles between an uncluttered screen and one with all
the shooting information shown. You can add 1 or 2
custom screens to these, so that the **Info** button now
toggles through 3 or 4 screens. The 2 screens offer the
same 3 options on each. This is because some
photographers might find the 3 extras all on one screen
rather confusing.

this is a histogram. It maps the brightness of
pixels in an image from black on the left to white on
the right and gives an indication of whether your
exposure is optimal. The image Olympus use for their
icon is a classically perfect histogram with no cut off
of the 'mountain range' on dark or light sides. This
represents an image with a dynamic range within the
capabilities of the sensor. On a sunlit day, the
difference in brightness between the deepest shadows
and the brightest whites (the dynamic range) may be
beyond the ability of the sensor to record it all. In this

image you can see the histogram bleeds off to the left. That means that there are gradation of black that cannot be coped with by the sensor at this exposure and they will be reproduced as all a uniform black. This may or may not matter, according to the amount of cut off and the detail contained in those pixels. You can bring those pixels within scope by increasing the exposure, which will move the entire range over to the right. There is a danger then that the brightest pixels will be out of the reproducible range(clipped). If so, the only option is a compromise to what seems to you the most attractive rendition.

**Highlights and Shadow** - this gives you a graphic representation of the areas of your picture that will be beyond the dynamic range, the range of brightness, that the Olympus E-M10 MkIII's sensor can encompass. Areas that are too dark to be reproduced (underexposed) are coloured blue, too light (overexposed) are coloured red

**Note:** in all of this, it should be remembered that there is no 'correct' exposure artistically. Correct exposure technically means reproducing the image with the least amount of clipping possible. Artistically, you may prefer the look of an image which is technically under or overexposed. Let your eyes be the ultimate judge of what is right pictorially. It is part of what distinguishes the work of one photographer from another.

**Level Gauge** - there is no quicker way to make an image look amateurish than tilting buildings or a wonky horizon. Olympus give you the chance to go straight with this option. It superimposes two bars on the screen which turn green when the image is straight horizontally and/ or vertically.

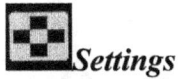*Settings*

If you go to **Playback** mode and turn the rear dial one click clockwise, you are presented with a grid view of all your images. This menu item lets you set how many images are presented to you at once plus, with further turns of the dial, which other screen you see (or not). If you have shot any **My Clips**, the time limited short video sequences, they can by viewed separately from still images and **Calendar** lets you select a date and see what images you made that day.

## Live View Boost

In normal shooting the camera gives you a view that is pretty much what the recorded image will look like, including any exposure compensation applied. In dim light, the image with negative compensation may be too dark to see properly. Set **Live View Boost** On and the camera concentrates on giving you a bright image. However, what you see on screen may not match the recorded image, since you will not see the effects of any exposure compensation.

## Flicker Reduction

Some forms of lighting induce a flickering effect on the EVF or monitor. **Auto** senses the problem and tries to lessen it. If that doesn't work, you can try the specific 50Hz and 60Hz settings. If you are in the USA, try 60Hz first, in Europe try 50Hz first. There's no reason to turn this **Off** so **Auto** is the obvious setting.

## Displayed Grid

This gives you a selection of grids that are overlaid on the screen. They don't appear on the image shot, of course. These are handy for checking you are straight on to building, for example, or accurate placement of objects in a composition. Appropriately, the 3rd grid down provides you with the points for the Rule of Thirds or Golden Mean. Cliche, maybe, but it works.

## **Peaking Color**

Choose the colour of edge outlining when using the **Peaking** focusing aid. The main thing is to use a colour that shows up clearly so you'll need to ring the changes as necessary.

# Custom C2. Disp /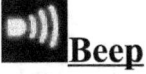/PC

## 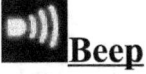Beep

This is another of Olympus's cryptic icons - it mean **Beep**. When the Olympus E-M10 MkIII locks on focus, it emits a high pitched beeping sound. If you don't like it or it is intrusive, this will switch it off.

## HDMI

You can connect the camera to a TV using an **HDMI** cable and view your images on the TV. If you have set your TV to 1080p, then set **1080p** here for example. You can also use the TV as a monitor when you are shooting a video. **Note:** the camera monitor blanks out when you are plugged in to a TV with **HDMI** On. Some TVs will allow you to control the Olympus E-M10 MkIII from their remote controls.

## USB Mode

The **USB** plug has several uses. Set to **Storage**, your camera is treated by your file explorer/ manager as a portable disk drive so you can move files around, delete them or copy/ transfer them to your PC or laptop. Set to **MTP** it appears as a device under your desktop. It enables you to do much the same as **Storage**. I find the **MTP** protocol a little flaky and prefer **Storage**.

### *Print*

You use this setting to print images directly from the camera.

press the **Playback** button and press OK

Scroll down the menu that appears to find 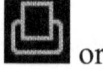 or
if you want to print all the images on your card.
If not, just scroll through the images pressing OK and
selecting the print icon for each one you want to print
Decide whether you want the **Date** and or **Time**
printed on each one or **No**
Plug the USB cable into a suitable printer and the
images will be printed
**Note:** to remove images from the print queue go
through them pressing the OK button and selecting
**Reset** or **Keep** as you desire.

## Custom D1. Exp/ISO/BULB

### Exposure Shift

This is one you are unlikely to want to use. For each

main **Metering** mode, **Digital ESP** , **Center**

**Weighted** and **Spot** you can adjust the
exposure in 1/6th of a stop increases by one stop each
way. This is not intended for amending the exposure
on a shot by shot bases like **Exposure Compensation**.
It is intended for use in case you find the Olympus E-
M10 MkIII is consistently under or over exposing in
all circumstances. It is extremely unlikely you will find
this the case because the Olympus metering is as good
as it gets. If, though, your personal taste is for a lighter
or darker image than Olympus's engineers have
arranged, here's where you can satisfy it. **Note:** this
setting does overlap with **Exposure Compensation** in
that if you set, say, -1 stop here, that you will only
have 4 stops **Exposure Compensation** available, -4
stops instead of -5. The same caveat applies with plus
settings too, of course.

### ISO-Auto Set

If choose **ISO Auto** in the main settings, the camera
will set the best **ISO** setting for you. If, in dim light
you prefer to use a longer shutter speed to take
advantage of the E-M10 MkIII's excellent stabilization
and thus keep the **ISO** down to prevent excessive
noise, this is where you can do it. The **Default Setting**
is best left at the camera's native sensitivity of 200
ISO. That ensures as noise free a performance as the
camera can achieve in reasonable light. The **High
Limit** should be set to the maximum **ISO** that you

consider has acceptable noise levels. I use 200ISO and 1600ISO as my settings. While I can accept the results at 3200/6400ISO for shooting in my dimly lit blues club, I do not find them acceptable for general work. At 1600ISO the E-M10 MkIII supplies image quality good enough for any of my routine needs.

## Noise Filter

When shooting at high **ISO** settings digital images become noisy, that is to say they exhibit random coloured specks caused by electronic noise. The higher the **ISO** the higher the noise. Digital cameras use several ploys to counteract this, including blurring the image. These anti-noise measures result in the image looking smoother but less detailed and sharp. The image quality losses entailed by using high ISOs are inevitable. This item enables you to choose your own preference for balancing detail and sharpness against graininess and speckling.

## Noise Reduct.

When you make a long exposure with a digital camera, the sensor itself generates noise internally. It is a fact of the technology. This noise can become very intrusive and spoil and image. If you set **Noise Reduct.** On, after you have taken your shot the camera makes another, blank exposure of the same length as the original. It uses this to know where the generated noise has occurred and thus where to correct the affected pixels in your picture. It only happens with exposures upwards of a second or so and will more than double the time it takes to take a picture. So, if your exposure is 10 seconds long, with **Noise Reduct.** it will take over 20 seconds to take and process before you can view it. It's a small price to pay for the image quality improvement it renders. You can set it **On** all the time but it slows the camera down unnecessarily and there is no point at faster shutter speeds. **Auto** is the best setting as the procedure will only take place when necessary. Custom D2. Exp/ISO/BULB

## Bulb/Time Timer

For this to work, the Mode dial must be set to **M**anual. This dictates the maximum time for which you can expose in **Bulb** or **Time**. The longest timed shutter speed on the E-M10 MkIII is 60 seconds. However, if you move the shutter speed beyond that you will come to **Bulb** or various flavours of **Time**. These allow for longer exposures than 60 seconds. **Bulb** and **Time** differ in that with **Bulb** you press the shutter and hold it down for as long as you wish to expose. With **Time** you press the shutter button once to start the exposure, then the shutter stays open until you press again. While you can regulate the exposure by pressing the shutter button, therefore, **Bulb/Time Timer** allows you to apply a time to them. Set it to 30 minutes and you have in effect set a shutter speed of 30 minutes. The camera will need a rigid support for these long exposure times.

## Live Bulb

See **Live Time** below.

## Live Time

While making your long exposure it is useful to get an idea of how it is building. In the past with **Bulb** or **Time** exposures, the screen went blank while the picture was taken so you could only see the result at the end of the exposure. The **Live** element here means that you may take a peek at the image several times as it is being built up. The number of peeks you are allowed is limited, however as it can impinge on image quality. For that reason, the lower the ISO, the more peeks you can have. The setting here is the interval between your screen view updates. This is quite a facility to have because if you judge an exposure of 8 minutes at /5.6 with a screen update every 30 seconds, if the image is to your liking at the 10th update, you can press the shutter button again and end the exposure. The panel that opens up at the bottom left of the display is a histogram, built up as the exposure progresses. Since the first period of time will be the image building up from nothing, the pixel distribution will all be to the left, the shadow side. As the image builds, the histogram will move to the right. Because night photographs usually have contrasty lighting from small sources like street lamps a histogram will rarely look like the classic 'normal' exposure, one of a central hill tapering off to the sides, and so the monitor image and your eyes are a better criterion.

## Composite Settings

Composite here refers to adding elements of the developing **Time** image exposure to the to the image so far. Thus, if there is a street lamp in an image, it will be exposed once until it is correctly exposed, at which point, as the exposure progresses it will be ignored. However, if another street lamp comes on in another area of the image, that will be added to the image which will now show both lights. And so on. The classic use of this would be a firework display. No matter how many fireworks go off they will only be added to the image if they make the area of the screen where they appear brighter than previously. Gradually you build up an image where the entire sky is a dazzling mass of exploding fireworks. The **Composite Setting** itself determines the base exposure of your image. If the fireworks are being set off behind a floodlit castle will need to set a proper exposure for the wall because that will be there all through the exposure and needs to be properly exposed for the picture to succeed. So if the camera is set to f/4 and the castle wall requires an exposure of 1 second at f/4, set the **Composite Setting** accordingly. Now, the castle wall will be exposed at the start of the exposure and will not change as the fireworks are gradually added (composited). The **Composite Exposure** forms the base exposure for your image, in other words.

# Custom E. Custom

## X Sync

this sets the maximum shutter speed that can be used when the flash is fitted and turned on. The top speed is limited to 1/250th for technical reasons to do with the focal plane shutter that all Micro Four Thirds cameras use. You have options from 1/60th to 1/250. If you have a moving subject with fairly bright ambient light and use a slower shutter speed you can get a double imaging effect due to the mixing of the flash and ambient light. When your main light source is the flash, therefore, it makes sense to use the highest 1/250th speed to eliminate as much as possible of the ambient light. A consequence of eliminating the ambient light is that while the foreground of your picture will be properly exposed by the flash, the background, being further away from the light source, will be underexposed. Which is the reason that not only can you set the highest speed the camera will use but also the lowest - see **Slow Limit** below. **Note:** the **X-Sync** setting applies to **P**, **A**, **S** and **M** modes. In **iAuto** all decisions are made by the camera.

## Slow Limit

This sets the slowest shutter speed the camera will use when flash is being used. While **X-Sync**, the top limit, applies to all shooting modes, **Slow Limit** applies only to **P** and **A**. In **S** and **M** modes, you can set any shutter speed you wish regardless. **Note:** Some examples are necessary here. I will assume that you have set **X-Sync** at 1/250th in all cases.

You are taking party pictures at night indoors and just want well lit sharp pictures of your friends in front of the camera, dancing and fooling around. Use **A** or **P** mode and set a **Slow Limit** of 1/250th. Set the aperture to f/5.6. All your pictures will be taken at 1/250th at f5.6, in the dark room making the flash effectively the only light source. Your pictures will be sharp and well lit while the background will be dark, focusing attention on your subjects

In the same scenario as above but while you still want your subjects sharp and clear, you'd like to be able to see some room atmosphere as well. Without flash, the room lighting would require an exposure of about 1/15th at f/4 which would render the dancing revellers very blurred. Use **A** mode. Set the aperture to f/4 and **Slow Limit** to 1/30th. You will have sharp and well lit friends but if they are dancing there may be some double imaging/ blurring. This can be regarded as give some atmosphere to the shots if the blurring is not too great. It is an effect which can certainly be used creatively. You could set **Slow Limit** to 1/15th or even lower to use all the room's available lighting but then since you are hand holding the camera you'd run the risk of adding camera shake to the mix

You are taking a portrait in a well lit office. The office has strip lighting which is very unflattering to your subject. You want your portrait to show the subject's working environment and so require a great depth of focus to get the both subject and background sharp. The light level of the room is 1/30th at f/2.8. Use **A** mode. Set the **Slow Limit** to 1 second. You will need to use a tripod for this shot. Set the aperture to f/11. The camera will set the shutter speed to about 1/2 second. Ask your subject to keep still! The camera fire the flash strongly enough to light the subject properly while adjusting the shutter to speed to suit the room light

In the last two scenarios using long exposures you could equally well use **S** or **M** modes and set the slow shutter speed explicitly since those modes ignore the **Slow Limit** setting. The advantage of using **A** combined with **Slow Limit** is that you have control of the aperture and thus depth of field while the camera takes care of the shutter speed. If you set the shutter speed explicitly, the camera takes care of the aperture in a situation where the depth of field is your primary creative control.

### Flash+Exposure Compensation

Normally any **Exposure Compensation** applied affects only ambient light. So, if you were making a flash portrait at 1/60 second at f/4, balancing the room and flash lighting and you dialled in +1 **Exposure Compensation**, the flash exposure would remain the same but the ambient light would be upped one stop, lightening the background. With this set **On**, the room would still be lightened but the flash exposure on the face would be adjusted upwards at the same time. The time to use this would be if you were finding your overall scene brightness too low. **Note:** On the **SCP** there is a flash intensity control so I prefer to leave this item **Off** and manipulate my flash exposure, if necessary, independently of the background from there.

### +WB

If you have manually set **White Balance** to (tungsten), if you take a flash shot it will come out with a bright blue cast. This setting avoids that by automatically setting the **WB** to **Auto** or **Flash** when the flash is activated. It doesn't alter the setting shown on the **SCP** while the flash is being used and it reverts to your own setting when the flash is deactivated. It is hard to think of a reason to turn this **Off** unless you want a colour cast for creative purposes.

## Custom F. 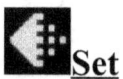/WB/Color

### 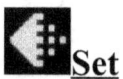Set

This obscure icon means "Image Quality" - No, me neither It applies to the **JPG** files recorded by the camera. There are too many combinations of **JPG** quality and image size to list on the **SCP** or Live Control screens, so the purpose of this menu item is to choose the four settings that you want to see displayed. **Note:** A brief explanation of **JPG** compression and file sizes might be handy. The uncompressed file sizes direct from digital camera sensors are large, making them unwieldy to store and process. A **RAW** file from the E-M10 MkIII comes in at about 14MB. The same pixel dimension **JPG** version might come in at 25% of that or even less depending on the subject. That is because the file is **compressed**. In its simplest form, let's say a blue sky takes up half of your picture. That blue sky is not in nature as uniform as it might look to the eye and the camera will record many levels of blue in it. **JPG** compression examines the area of blue and instead of storing each pixel separately, maybe 5000 pixels, it stores one typical level of blue and a note to repeat it 1000 times. This loses the subtle nuances of blue in the original but the **JPG** compression takes account of the human eye's perception of blue and to all intents and purposes it is identical. Of course, the more you apply compression, the approximation you get and the less accurate the image. At very high compressions, unpleasant compression artefacts can be seen, often as a kind of halo around the edges of objects in the image. There is another way to save an image with a smaller file size and that is to make the image physically smaller. A full size Olympus E-M10

MkIII image is 4608x3456 = 15,925,248 pixels total. Reduce that to 1280x960 = 1,228,800 pixels and you have a massive saving in size. The E-M10 MkIII offers **JPG** compression at four levels, **S**uper **F**ine, **F**ine, **N**ormal and **B**asic and image sizes **L**arge 4608x3456, **M**edium 3200x2400 and **S**mall1280x960. I'd suggest using as below

**LSF** for all normal shooting. You can discard detail from a large file by compress more or reducing image size in post processing but you cannot add detail that is not present because a small file size or heavy compression has discarded it

**MF or MN** is good enough for emailing

**SN** or **SB** is enough for social media

I'd suggest **LSF MSF SN** and **SB** for settings here. (**SB** for when using the camera as a notebook, taking a picture of where your car is parked, for example)

**Note:** You will see these choices in the four **RAW+JPG** settings too. It is a counsel of perfection but I am an advocate of always shooting a **RAW** file. As processing and noise algorithms improve, they can be applied to your **RAW** pictures so that even your old pictures can be displayed with the latest and greatest noise and other settings applied. The camera always works from a **RAW** file initially but when you set the **Image Quality** to any **JPG** only setting, the **RAW** file is discarded once the **JPG** is made. When you view a **RAW** file in **Playback** you are not looking at the **RAW** file itself but a small **JPG** embedded in it automatically for viewing only.

## WB

This is related to the colour temperature, redness or blueness, of the ambient light. It only applies to **JPG** files. For **RAW** files **Auto** is fine for all conditions since you can set the **White Balance** in post processing. **Auto** works very effectively for **JPG** as well and is the best choice for everyday use. It is not omnipotent, however and sometimes you get a better, more accurate result by setting the **White Balance** explicitly. In reality, it often comes down to trial and error. If none of the built in settings works for you, you can set a **Custom WB**. You can set a **CustomWB** using One **Touch White Balance** as described below or manually. To set a **Custom** balance follow this procedure.

Place a sheet of white paper or card where you can easily photograph it in the same lighting that will be used for your picture

Press the **Shortcut** button or **OK** and select the **WB** setting

Scroll with the front dial until you reach **CustomWB**

Press Info and photograph your sheet of white paper. Ideally the white paper should fill the frame. It doesn't matter if it is in focus or not when it fills the frame

A **Yes/No** dialog appears. If your sheet of paper looks white, choose **Yes** to save the setting. You can save up to four **CustomWB** settings for reuse when you are using the lighting again

To set a **CustomWB** manually use the same procedure as above but in step 2 press **OK** instead of **Info**. You can then manipulate the **WB** using two sliders. It is quite difficult to judge and would only be useful if the method above didn't provide good results. I've never some across such a situation. **Note: WB** settings are necessary because while the human eye adapts to the ambient light conditions without us perceiving it, the camera does not. A piece of white paper viewed in shade on a sunny day or in the open at sunset still looks white to the human eye. Actually, objectively measured, it is quite blue under the tree and quite red under sunset conditions and that is how the camera would portray it if left to its own devices. **WB** is how the camera keeps whites white when it records an image. If you are shooting **RAW**, you can adjust the WB however you wish in post processing. **White Balance** is measured in degrees Kelvin, the lower the number the redder (warmer) the light, the higher the number the bluer (colder) the light. Candlelight is about the warmest light you'd normally encounter and is in the 1000k to 2000k range, a clear sunny day is 5000 to 6500k and on a clear sunny day but in the shade 9000k to 10000k. A sunset might be around 3000k. What makes **WB** tricky is illustrated by the latter setting. If you set **WB** for the sunset to 3000k, a white will look white in your picture. But the reason we love a sunset is largely the sheer spectacular redness, the warmth of everything. We want it to be red. I say this not to confuse but to illustrate that the white balance, like so much in photography, is not totally a matter of correct or incorrect but an artistic judgement as well.

## WB Auto Keep Warm Color

If you are shooting under incandescent light, that is lights which work by heating a filament rather than low energy types, you may find the colours too warm. In which case, set this to **Off**. I prefer the warmer rendering of **On**. This does not affect results under other lighting conditions.

## Color Space

This affects only **JPG** files. It does not affect the range or number of colours captured by the sensor. **sRGB** is the accepted standard for almost every application and every display medium understands it.

**Adobe RGB** is really a specialist professional standard which in theory has a wider colour range. However, used on normal display media, it leads to rather dull colours being displayed. It exists because in some professional fields they prefer to be given the wider range of colours so that they can tailor them to the colour space they prefer for their particular use or client preference. There is no gain and some disadvantage in using **Adobe RGB** unless you have a specific reason to do so.

**sRGB** being the accepted standard for digital displays, outputting your images to that space gives you the best chance of viewers seeing your image as you intended In the case of **RAW** files, you assign a **Color Space** of your choice when exporting to **JPG** so the setting here does not matter. **Note:** color space needs explaining. A camera sensor can capture far many more colours than any monitor or other viewing medium can display. However, in order to look convincing most images must have a range of colours spanning from black through to white. So we have a sensor capable of supplying, say, 20 million colours and a display medium capable of showing only 10 million of them. The output of the sensor must somehow be matched to the ability of the display medium. **Color Space** is how it is done. If you output to **Adobe RGB** you need to be sure that your image will be viewed on a display that understands and can use it. If it does not, the display will interpret the colours as best it can, the result often being a rather low contrast and lifeless image. In reality, the appearance of your image is always a hostage to fortune unless every step of the chain from your camera to every viewer's viewing device is calibrated.

# Custom G. Record

## File Name

### *Auto*

As you take pictures, they are numbered so if you take 5 pictures they will go from 0001 to 0005. If you insert a new card the numbering will continue from 0006 and so on. When you import the camera files to your computer, there will be no filename clashes.

### *Reset*

if you insert a new card file names will start at the next number from the highest so like **Auto**, if you have 5 images, the next one will be 0006. However, if you insert a new card, file names will recommence at 0001. Unless you have a reason not to, **Auto** seems the sensible choice.

## Edit Filename

This lets you edit the first characters of the filename assigned by the camera. You can choose the first 4 characters of the filename for **sRGB** while for **Adobe RGB** a mandatory underscore is added and you can choose the next 3 characters.

## Copyright Settings

here you can set **Artist Name** and **Copyright Name** which will be written into the EXIF (Exchangeable Image File Format). In these days of wholesale copyright infringement, at least the thief cannot plead that he didn't know the image was copyright - for what it's worth.

# Custom H. EVF

## EVF Auto Switch

With this set to **On**, the camera will sense when your
eye is at the **EVF** and turn it on, shutting down the
monitor to save the battery. Take your eye from the
**EVF** and it turns off and transfers viewing to the
monitor. If you turn this **Off** you will need to switch
between them manually using the **Monitor** button on
the right side of the **EVF** housing. You'd normally
leave this on **Auto** but manual switching can be helpful
when the camera is on a tripod and you alter some
settings on the camera. It is quite easy while doing so
to brush the **Auto** sensor unintentionally and switch
the monitor off. Another use would be for street
photography where you know you will be using the
**EVF** and don't want to wait for the short delay while
the camera switches on the **EVF**.

## EVF Adjust

This enables you to tailor the **EVF** brightness and hue
to your preferences if you feel the need. **EVF Auto
Luminance** With this On, the camera adjusts the
brightness automatically. **EVF Adjust** When you
select this, the monitor turns off and the brightness and
hue adjustments appear in the **EVF** itself so that you
can judge the effect. If you have **EVF Auto
Luminance** set **On**, the camera is taking care of
brightness and you can only adjust the hue
temperature. The Olympus E-M10 MkIII has a nicely
bright and detailed **EVF** and I've never found any need
to change its default settings.

## Custom I. Utility

### <u>Pixel Mapping</u>

This checks and if necessary corrects any anomalies in the camera's sensor and image processing functions. Unless you notice something amiss, there's not a lot of point in using this. If you do use it, leave the camera on for a minute or two so that the sensor warms up.

### <u>Level Adjust</u>

If you find the **Level Gauge** is inaccurate, you can adjust it here. Make sure the camera is set absolutely level, select **Adjust** and press **OK**. If that looks worse, you can **Reset** it to its default. You can buy spirit levels that fit in the flash hotshoe if you do need to reset this. Or otherwise, mount the camera on a tripod with a spirit level.

### <u>Touchscreen Settings</u>

Enable or disable the Touchscreen. Disabled, you will only be able to select parameters to alter from the **SCP** using the rear dial plus touch focusing and shutter operation will be disabled. Useful if you find your nose changes settings while you have your eye to the EVF. **Note:** when you have the touchscreen turned on with information showing (press the **INFO** button) you can control the touch operations with three icons on the left of the screen which you can cycle through with a tap of

the finger. , the camera will focus where you

touch the screen and then fire the shutter. the
camera will focus where you touch but you must

release the shutter as normal. the touch screen is **Off** overriding **Touchscreen Settings.**

## Sleep

This simply sets how long the camera will stay ready for action with the monitor active before it turns off the monitor to save battery power. The shorter the **Sleep** time the longer the battery will last. I make it a habit to turn the camera **Off** while I am carrying it. It switches back on ready for use in a second or so, so there's no need to leave it on all the time you are out and about. If you turn **Sleep Off**, the camera will stay ready for action for 4 hours. If unused in for that time, it will switch itself **Off**. In that case, the **On/Off** lever will be in the **On** position, though the camera is **Off**. Switch it **Off** and then **On** again to restart it.

## Eye-Fi

Eye-Fi cards allow you to upload files via the card's own built in Wi-Fi. Since you can now connect the camera via normal Wi-Fi to a network or a smartphone,Eye-Fi is now effectively redundant for Micro Four Thirds cameras.

## Certification

This displays the certification icons. I have no idea what they are for or what they mean, though the triangular one may mean that you should not machine wash the Olympus E-M10 MkIII. I presume that means that the camera can be dry cleaned. Personally, I find a damp micro-fibre cloth works well enough.

# Setup

## Card Setup

### All Erase

This will simply erase all the images on your card. However, If you have protected any images they will not be erased.

### Format

This sets up an SD card ready for use in the camera. If you buy a new card, the first thing to do is to **Format** it in camera. Similarly, If a card is giving you problems of any kind, this is the first thing to try in order to remedy it. **Format** deletes all the images on the card, protected or not! **Note:** images are protected in **Playback** grid view by touching the tab at the bottom of the screen where you will see a key symbol. Highlight the image you want to protect by scrolling through them with the front dial and touching the key icon. If you are viewing a single image, touching it will bring up the key icon at the bottom of the screen

## Time

Set the camera's time. This is the time stamp that will be saved with files (and printed on them if you so wish).

## Language

Set the desired language for the menu.

## Monitor Adjustment

You can adjust the **Colour Temperature** and **Brightness** of the monitor here. **Colour Temperature** will only apply in Playback but **Brighness** is an overall setting. It is unlikely you will need to alter either of these but if you decide to change the **Colour Temperature** you can do it while viewing an image in **Playback** mode. That will enable you to see the effect. Plus gives more blue. Minus more red. It doesn't alter the image itself.

## Rec View

This applies to what happens after you take a picture. Set to any of the time settings, the image will be automatically displayed on the monitor for that amount of time after it is taken, reverting to normal operation after that. You don't have to view it for that long. A touch on the shutter button returns the camera to normal operation. Set to **Auto**, the image is simply held on screen until you touch the shutter button. Set **Off**, the image is not displayed after taking at all. You can view it at any time by pressing the **Playback** button, of course.

## WiFi Settings

These apply to setting the camera up to connect to your smartphone using the free Olympus Image Share app. Once set up the app enables you to control the E-M10 MkIII remotely, upload images from the camera to your phone for social media use, for example and to Geotag location information to your pictures.

### Wi_Fi Connect Settings

**Private** will be the most used here. Having connected to your phone once, using **Private** it will connect automatically thereafter. **One-Time** provides for a one off connection to a friend or colleague's smartphone and must be assigned anew for each connection. **Off** simply switches off the Wi-Fi connection.

*Private Password*

This supplies the password for use with **One-Time** connection.

*Reset Share Order*

Setting a **Share Order** on an image by pressing in **Playback** mode tells the camera to copy them to your smartphone without further notice when a **Wi-Fi** connection is made. If you have set any images as a **Share Order**, setting this to **Yes** will cancel them.

*Reset Wi-Fi Settings*

if you change your smartphone or make a hash of connecting to it, this sets you back to square one so that you can start again.

## Firmware

This tells you the **Firmware** version you are using on your camera and lens. Olympus have a policy of constantly improving and upgrading their camera and lens performance by releasing updates. You can update a Panasonic lens's firmware while it is mounted on an Olympus camera. **Note:** Olympus have made upgrading their firmware into a simple and reliable procedure. Go to their website and download the **Olympus Digital Camera Updater** and run it. Make sure your USB Connection is set to **Storage** (**Custom** menu **C2**) and plug your camera into your computer via the **USB** port. The camera will connect and a press on**Firmware Upgrade** will talk you through the procedure. Make sure you have plenty of charge in the battery before doing this.

# My Example Menu

These are my choices so may not suit you but they will give you a working basis on which to start. If you have been altering the setup a lot it will be worth doing a full reset before starting.

## Shooting Menu 1

**Reset** - N/A
**Picture Mode** - Natural (3)
**Digital Tele-converter** - Off
**Metering** -

## Shooting Menu 2

**Image Stabilizer** - S-IS On
**AF Illuminator** - On
Elec.Zoom Speed - Normal
- 0.0
**Intrvl.Sh./Time Lapse** - Off
**RC Mode** - Off

## Video Menu

**Movie (sound)** - On
**Recording Volume** - 0
**AF Mode** - S-AF
**Image Stabilizer** - M-IS 2
**Elec.Zoom Speed** - Normal
**Video Frame Rate** - 25p (30p USA)
**Video Bit rate** - Fine

## Playback Menu

**(Slide Show)** - As preferred
**(Image Rotation)** - On
**Edit** - N/A
**Print Order** - N/A
**Reset Protect** - N/A

**Connection to Smartphone** - N/A

## Custom A AF/MF
**AEL/AFL** - Mode1/ Mode2/ Mode3
**AF Targeting Pad** - On
**Face Priority** - Off
**MF Assist** - Magnify On Peaking On
**Reset Lens** - Off

## Custom B. Button/Dial
**Fn1** - AEL/AFL
**Fn2** - Magnify (for precise focusing position)

## Custom C1 Disp/Sound/PC
**Control Settings** - All LV-C N/A
**Info Settings** - Playback Info Image Only + Overall
**ticked** - LV-Info Custom 1 & 2 ticked - Playback
**Settings** - 25/MyClips/Calendar
**Live View Boost** - Off
**Flicker Reduction** - Auto
**Displayed Grid** - Off
**Peaking Colour** - Red

## Custom C2 Disp/Sound/PC
**Beep** - On
**HDMI** - 1080p/ Off
**USB Mode** - Auto

## Custom D1 Exp/ISO/BULB
**Exposure Shift** - All 0
**ISO Auto Set** - 3200/ 200
**Noise Filter** - Low
**Noise Reduct.** - Auto

## Custom D2 Exp/ISO/BULB
**Bulb/Time Timer** - 8min
**Live Bulb** - Off

**Live Time** - As applicable. For a 1 minute exposure, I'd use 8 second intervals

**Composite Settings** - As applicable. Essentially, this is the exposure for your basic picture before you start adding fireworks, stars or what have you

## E. (Flash) Custom

**X-Sync** - 1/250
**Slow Limit** - 1/60
**Flash Compensation+Exposure Compensation** - Off
**Flash+WB** - WB Auto

## Custom F. JPG Quality/WB/Sound/PC

**Quality Set** - LSF MSF SN SB
**WB** - Auto
**Keep Warm color** - On
**Color Space** - sRGB

## G. Record

**File Name** - Auto
**Edit File Name** - To choice
**Copyright Settings** - On (your name as Artist and Copyright normally)

## Custom H. EVF

**EVF Auto Switch** - On
**EVF Adjust** - 0 0 (default)

## Custom I. Utility

**Pixel Mapping** - N/A
**Level Adjust** - N/A
**Touchscreen Settings** - On
**Sleep** - On
**Eye-Fi** - On if you have an Eye-Fi card
**Certification** - N/A

## HDR example

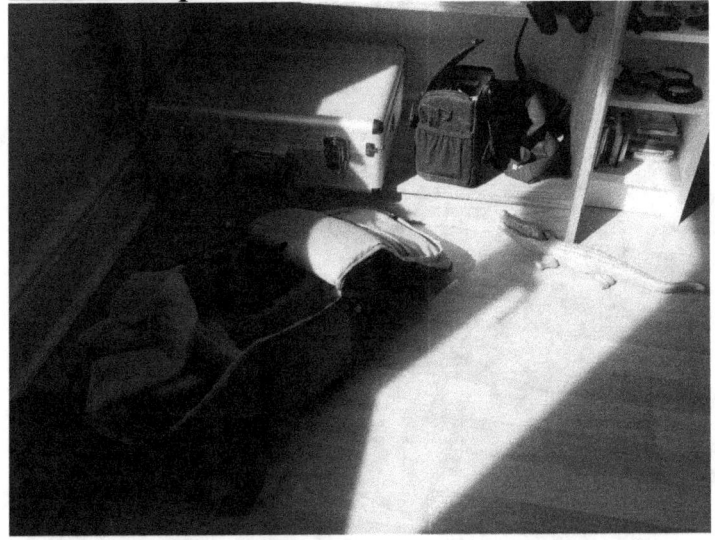

A scene containing both black and silver objects is a test for any camera's dynamic range. Those extremes of reflectance half lit by a shaft of bright direct sunlight as in this picture exceed any camera's ability to capture them in one picture. Add enough plus exposure compensation to capture detail in the shadows and the highlights burn out. Add enough minus compensation to capture highlight detail and the dark areas go murky. The only answer is **H**igh **D**ynamic **R**ange photography, which shoots two or more frames at different exposures and combines them to try to get the best of both worlds. The problem is that the screen or photo paper that you view the image on has a limited range too. So, in order to display the HDR image the colour range must be compressed - which can lead to a rather flat and often unreal rendering of the image. In a case like the one here, which image is best is, in the end, a matter of personal taste.

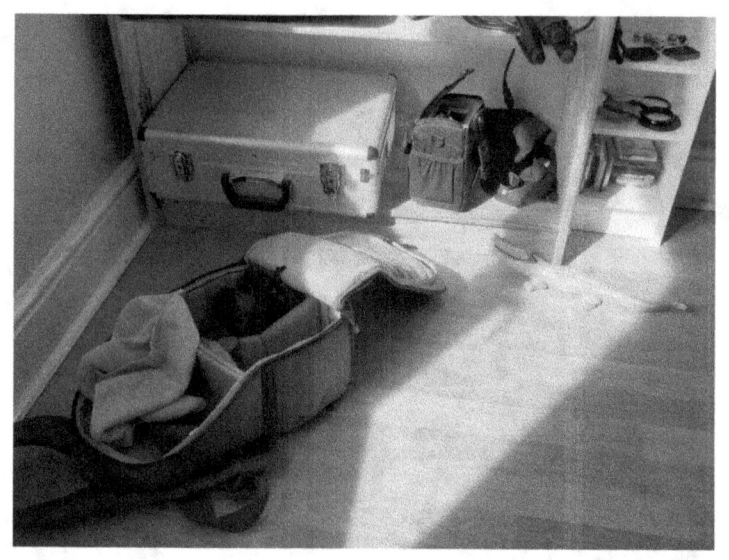

## **Jello Effect example**

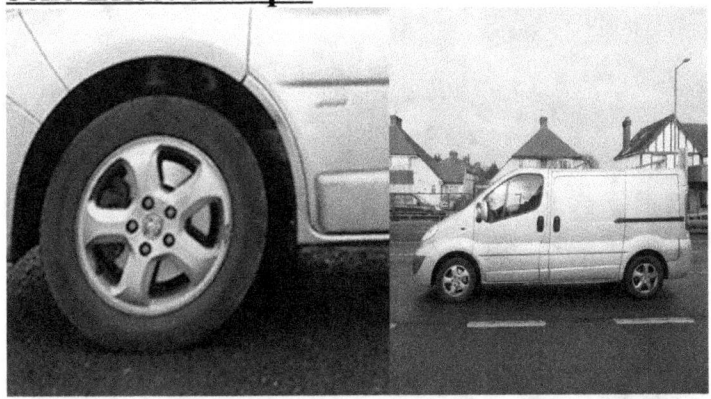

The 'Jello' effect is a well known disadvantage of the way that electronic shutters work. It is caused by the image being captured by a live sequential scan of the sensor rather than all at once by using a normal shutter, You can see the effect at its worst in the picture above. Note the oval wheel and the 'leaning back' appearance of the van. While the effect used to be very marked, it is minimized by the much faster scan now possible with this camera's formidable processing power. My picture is taken to deliberately highlight the effect. In day to day photography you would not often notice it.

# Keystone Comp example

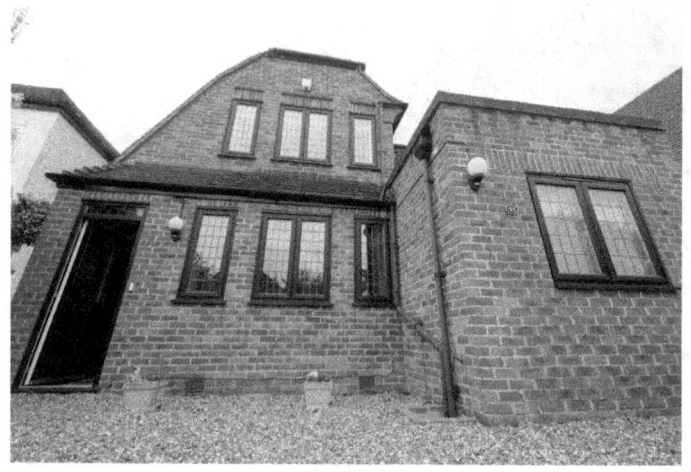

This shot had to be taken on a very wide angle lens because of a lack of space at the front of the house. The rather extreme converging verticals effect renders the picture less than ideal. The problem is that when the human eye sees something like this in real life, the brain compensates for the effect but it cannot do so for an image. Luckily the camera will do what your brain cannot! The image below is with Keystone Comp. near the extremes of its correction. **Note:** Panasonic 7-14mm zoom @ 9mm, 125th @ f/5.6 ISO 400 and +1/3 exposure compensation.

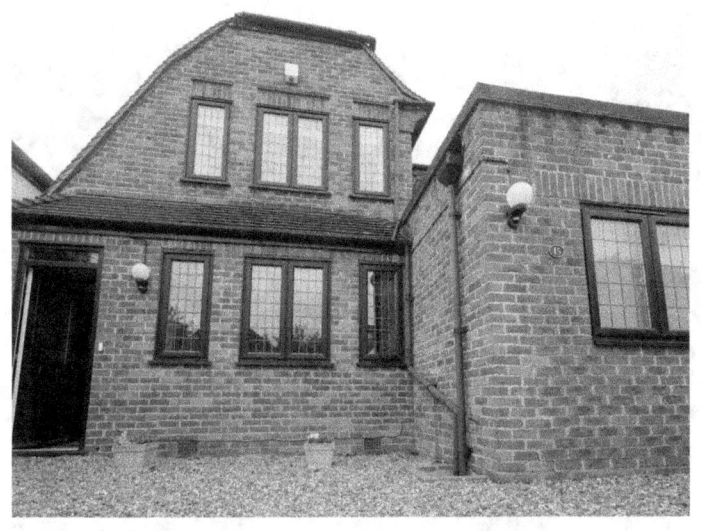

## <u>Multiple Exposure example</u>

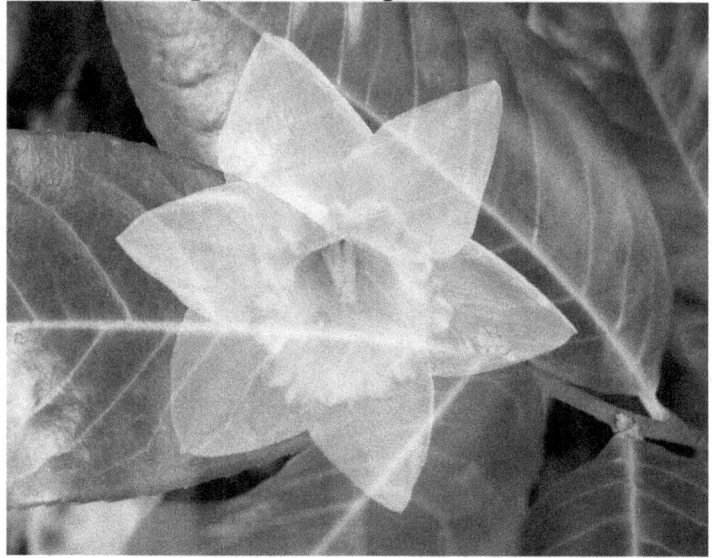

There's a lot of fun to be had with **Multiple Exposure** and little excuse not to try the technique now that it is so easily done in camera with the E-M10 MkIII using Here I express my deep commitment to nature, my garden and the miracle of Spring. Well, ok, I was just messing about because the E-M10 MkIII makes it so easy!

## **<u>Flash Sync example</u>**

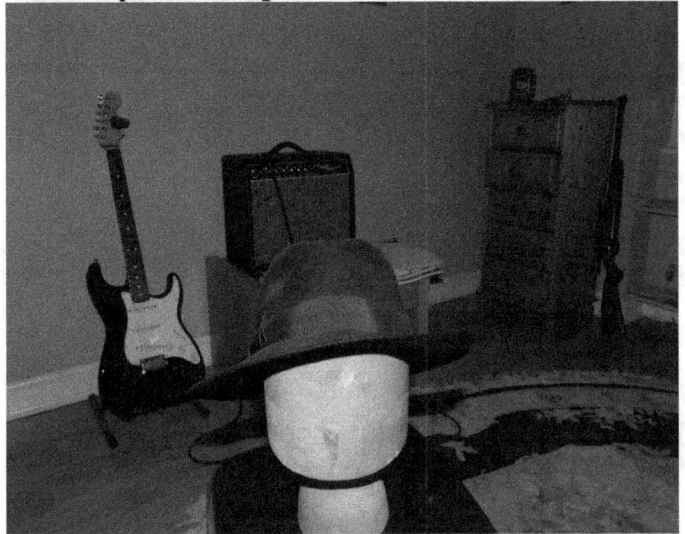

Using a slow shutter speed with flash gives you great control over how a flash image will look. In both these shots, I have used Aperture priority and f/11 to get enough depth of field. In the first shot, I have set the shutter speed **Slow Limit** for the flash to 1/250th as I normally would, to avoid mixing flash with daylight and getting a blurred or double imaged exposure. For the shot below, I set the shutter speed Slow Limit to 1 second because I knew I was going to be using a tripod. The camera has made a perfect job of balancing flash and daylight to give me an evenly lit foreground plus detail in the background. It set a shutter speed of 1/3 second.

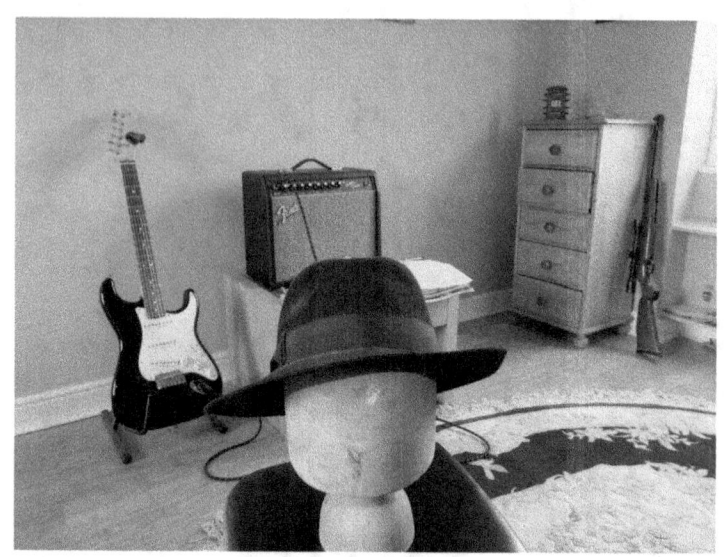

## <u>Stabilization example</u>

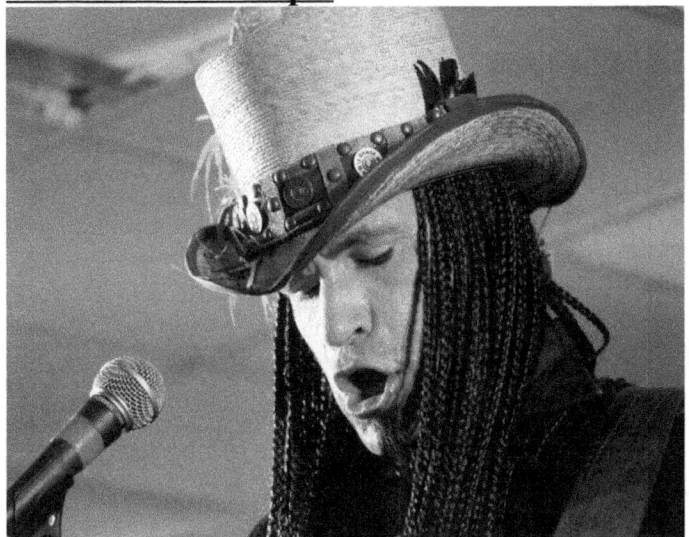

Olympus cameras have long been known for having the best in body stabilization in the business. My shot here is in a dark blues club (blues clubs ought to be dark and preferably dingy too!). This is at 1/60th @ f/2.8, ISO6400 on the 40-150mm f/2.8 Pro zoom at 150mm. Without stabilization the recommended shutter speed would be 1/600th. I would be surprised to find more than 10% of my shots at this speed to be less than sharp and some of those would be due to subject movement or lack of depth of field.

# Table of Contents